The MAILBOX®
The Education Center®

# Math
## Choose & Do Grids

## Over 375 Differentiated Activities

**42 grids! 42 practice pages!**

- Number sense
- Computation
- Fractions
- Algebra and Patterns
- Measurement
- Problem solving
- and more!

*Skill practice that gives students choices!*

**Managing Editor:** Jennifer Bragg

**Editorial Team:** Becky S. Andrews, Diane Badden, Kimberley Bruck, Karen A. Brudnak, Chris Curry, Tazmen Hansen, Marsha Heim, Lori Z. Henry, Njeri Legrand, Debra Liverman, Kitty Lowrance, Laura Mihalenko, Jennifer Nunn, Mark Rainey, Hope Rodgers, Rebecca Saunders, Hope Taylor Spencer, Rachael Traylor, Sharon M. Tresino, Zane Williard

## www.themailbox.com

©2010 The Mailbox® Books
All rights reserved.
ISBN10 #1-56234-947-3 • ISBN13 #978-1-56234-947-9

Printed in the United States
10 9 8 7 6 5 4 3 2 1

HPS 215497

# What's

**Two simple steps!**

1. **Program** the student directions.
2. **Copy** the grid and its practice page.

**Address different learning levels and styles with a single grid!**

## Multiplication Facts (0–5)

Name _____

Date _____

Choose ___ or more activities to do.
When you finish an activity, color its number.

| | | |
|---|---|---|
| **1** Color nine arrays on graph paper. Show each multiplication fact from 4 x 1 to 4 x 9.<br><br>4 x 2 = 8 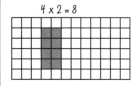 | **2** Draw pictures to show that each pair of facts has the same product.<br><br><table><tr><td>2 x 3<br>3 x 2</td><td>1 x 5<br>5 x 1</td></tr><tr><td>3 x 4<br>4 x 3</td><td>4 x 2<br>2 x 4</td></tr></table> | **3** Copy and complete the problems. Then write a rule for multiplying by 1.<br><br>0 x 1 = ___     ___ x 1 = 1<br><br>2 x ___ = 2     ___ x 1 = 3<br><br>4 x 1 = ___     5 x ___ = 5 |
| **4** How can skip-counting help you solve a multiplication problem? List your ideas and then share them with a friend. | **5** Do the practice page "Exactly Even."  | **6** Order the words to tell the zero property. Write the sentence.<br><br><table><tr><td>number</td><td>Any</td></tr><tr><td>multiplied</td><td>equals</td></tr><tr><td>zero</td><td>zero.</td><td>by</td></tr></table><br>Write five facts that prove this property. |
| **7** Copy and complete the table.<br><br>| x | 0 | 1 | 2 | 3 | 4 | 5 |<br>|---|---|---|---|---|---|---|<br>| 0 | | | | | | |<br>| 1 | | | | | | |<br>| 2 | | | | | | |<br>| 3 | | | | | | |<br>| 4 | | | | | | |<br>| 5 | | | | | | | | **8** Write three or more ways to find the total number of fingers.  | **9** Write 16 facts. Multiply each number in column A by each number in column B.<br><br>| A | B |<br>|---|---|<br>| 2 | 6 |<br>| 3 | 7 |<br>| 4 | 8 |<br>| 5 | 9 | |

**Note to the teacher:** Program the student directions with the number of activities to be completed. Then copy the page and page 30 (back-to-back if desired) for each student.

# Inside

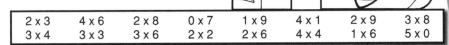

## Multiplication Facts (0–5)

Name_____   Date_____

### Exactly Even

Write two problems from the box
on each balance scale.
Mark off the problems in the box.

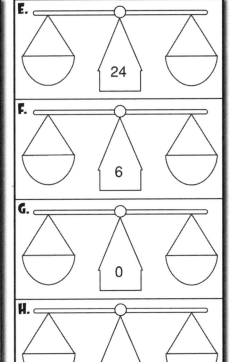

| 2 x 3 | 4 x 6 | 2 x 8 | 0 x 7 | 1 x 9 | 4 x 1 | 2 x 9 | 3 x 8 |
| 3 x 4 | 3 x 3 | 3 x 6 | 2 x 2 | 2 x 6 | 4 x 4 | 1 x 6 | 5 x 0 |

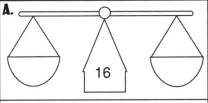

**A.** 16

**E.** 24

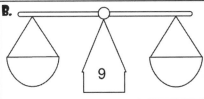

**B.** 9

**F.** 6

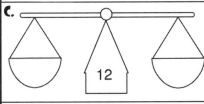

**C.** 12

**G.** 0

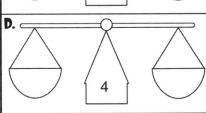

**D.** 4

**H.** 18

*Choose & Do Math Grids* • ©The Mailbox® Books •

30   **Note to the teacher:** Use with page 29.

## Tip!
To save paper, copy a grid and its practice page back-to-back!

## Independent practice for

- Morning work
- Center work
- Homework
- Free time
- Anytime

**Answer keys on pages 90–96.**

# Table of Contents

## Number Sense

## Addition and Subtraction

## Multiplication and Division

## Measurement

## Algebra and Patterns

## Fractions

## Data Analysis

## Geometry

## Problem Solving

# Numbers to 999

Name _____

Date _____

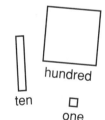

Choose ____ or more activities to do.
When you finish an activity, color its number.

| **1** | Work with a classmate. Take turns counting by tens. Start counting at 456 and end at 726. Keep a list of the numbers said aloud. |
|---|---|

| **2** | Copy and complete the chart. |
|---|---|

| Hundreds | Tens | Ones | Number |
|---|---|---|---|
| four | three | two | |
| | nine | one | 791 |
| six | five | | 652 |
| eight | zero | three | |
| two | | seven | 237 |

**3** Write all the odd numbers in order from 35 to 79.

**4** Copy the chart. In each column, write three numbers. Use each digit (1–9) only once in each column.

| Numbers Less Than 96 | Numbers Greater Than 96 |
|---|---|
| | |
| | |

**5** Do the practice page "Batting Practice."

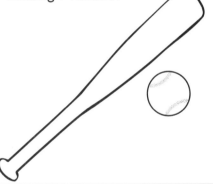

**6** Draw a model for each number.

| **13** | **103** | **130** |
|---|---|---|

How would the models change if 103 and 130 did not have zeros?

ten  hundred  one

**7** Write each number three different ways.

| 82 | 156 | 274 |
|---|---|---|
| 419 | 501 | 983 |

35 = thirty-five,
3 tens + 5 ones, 20 + 15

**8** First, use the digits 1, 4, and 8 to make six three-digit numbers. Then compare ten different number pairs.

418 < 481

**9** Copy the first number. Flip a coin. If it lands on heads, write the two numbers that come before the number. If it lands on tails, write the two numbers that come after the number. Repeat with each number.

| 36 | 21 | 79 | 42 |
|---|---|---|---|
| 89 | 93 | 65 | 54 | 17 |

**Note to the teacher:** Each student needs a coin to complete activity 9. Program the student directions with the number of activities to be completed. Then copy the page and page 6 (back-to-back if desired) for each student.

Name _____

Date _____

# Numbers to 999

## Batting Practice

Color the largest number in each group.
Compare the two uncolored numbers.

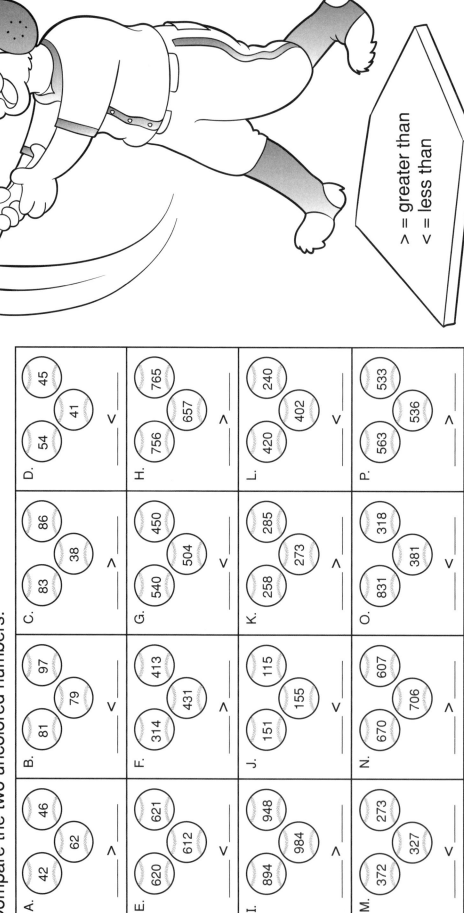

> = greater than
< = less than

A.
42  62
46
___ > ___

B.
81  79
97
___ < ___

C.
83  38
86
___ > ___

D.
54  41
45
___ < ___

E.
620  612
621
___ < ___

F.
314  431
413
___ > ___

G.
540  504
450
___ < ___

H.
756  657
765
___ > ___

I.
894  984
948
___ > ___

J.
151  155
115
___ < ___

K.
258  273
285
___ > ___

L.
420  402
240
___ < ___

M.
372  327
273
___ < ___

N.
670  706
607
___ > ___

O.
831  381
318
___ < ___

P.
563  536
533
___ > ___

**Note to the teacher:** Use with page 5.

# Numbers to 9,999

Name _____

Date _____

Choose ____ or more activities to do.
When you finish an activity, color its number.

**1** | Use the digits below to write six different numbers. Then rewrite the numbers from largest to smallest.

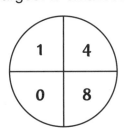

|   |   |
|---|---|
| 1 | 4 |
| 0 | 8 |

**2** | Cut eight cards. Write a different number from below on each card and circle the ones digit. Sort the cards into two groups: even and odd. Glue the groups on another sheet of paper and label them.

| 1,002 | 4,737 | 3,156 | 8,480 |
| 2,641 | 1,599 | 6,374 | 9,945 |

**3** | Copy and complete the chart.

| Number | + 10 | + 100 | + 1,000 |
|--------|------|-------|---------|
| 619 | 629 | 719 | 1,619 |
| 4,201 | | | |
| 35 | | | |
| 972 | | | |
| 5,614 | | | |

**4** | Write each number. Next to each number, write the value of the underlined digit.

| 4,2<u>8</u>5 | 7,<u>5</u>03 |
| 2,109 | 3,6<u>1</u>8 |
| 7,<u>6</u>39 | 1,72<u>4</u> |
| <u>8</u>,402 | 5,091 |

**5** | Do the practice page "Pop and Win!"

**6** | Draw the blanks and symbols on your paper. Roll a die eight times. Write the rolled numbers on the blanks to make two true comparisons. Repeat.

__, __ __ __ < __, __ __ __

__, __ __ __ > __, __ __ __

**7** | Copy the code. Use the symbols to draw 8 four-digit numbers. Ask a friend to name each number.

☐ = 1    ● = 10
▲ = 100    ◇ = 1,000

**8** | Draw a number line from 0 to 5,000. Mark each thousand with a line. Estimate where each number from below should go on the number line. Label each spot.

| 985 | 3,045 | 4,923 |
| 2,531 | 250 | 1,240 |

**9** | Softly count aloud by hundreds. Start at 1,734 and end at 3,034. Write each number you say.

**Note to the teacher:** Each student will need a die to complete activity 6. Program the student directions with the number of activities to be completed. Then copy the page and page 8 (back-to-back if desired) for each student.

7

8

Date _____

# Numbers to 9,999

## Pop and Win!

Color each balloon.
Use the code.

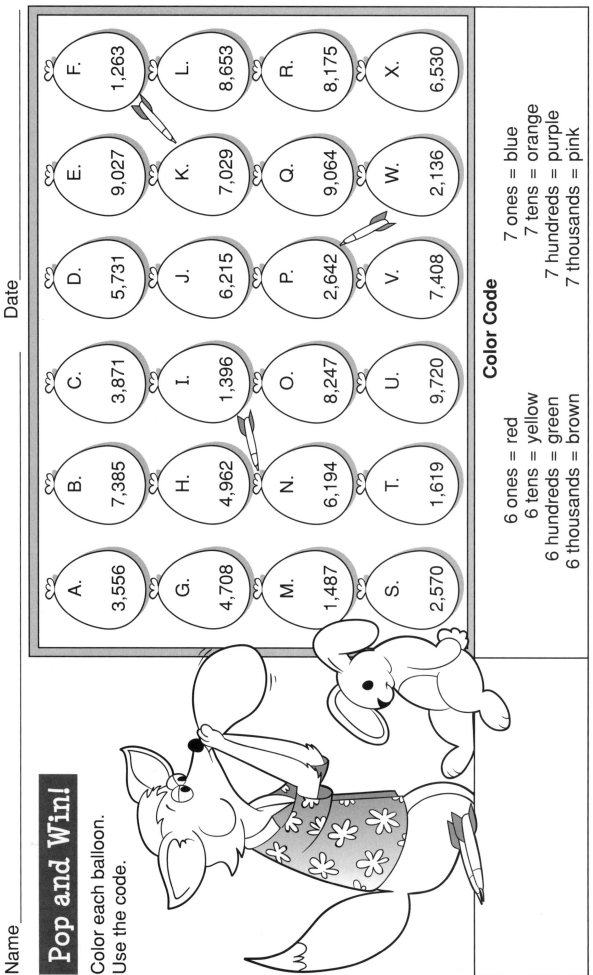

| | | | | | |
|---|---|---|---|---|---|
| A. 3,556 | B. 7,385 | C. 3,871 | D. 5,731 | E. 9,027 | F. 1,263 |
| G. 4,708 | H. 4,962 | I. 1,396 | J. 6,215 | K. 7,029 | L. 8,653 |
| M. 1,487 | N. 6,194 | O. 8,247 | P. 2,642 | Q. 9,064 | R. 8,175 |
| S. 2,570 | T. 1,619 | U. 9,720 | V. 7,408 | W. 2,136 | X. 6,530 |

## Color Code

6 ones = red
6 tens = yellow
6 hundreds = green
6 thousands = brown

7 ones = blue
7 tens = orange
7 hundreds = purple
7 thousands = pink

*Choose & Do Math Grids* • ©The Mailbox® Books • TEC61228 • Key p. 90

**Note to the teacher:** Use with page 7.

# Numbers to 99,999

Name _____

Date _____

Choose ____ or more activities to do.
When you finish an activity, color its number.

---

**1** Write each number on a different card. Use the cards to make the ten smallest five-digit numbers possible. Write each number you make.

| 5 | 7 | 2 | 6 | 9 |

**2** Round each number to the nearest hundred.

| 24,710 | 65,299 |
| 83,208 | 14,854 |
| 77,493 | 27,390 |
| 20,681 | 62,584 |

**3** Write each number in expanded form.

43, 219
86,745
18,875
37,021
56,940

---

**4** If 34,☐17 > 34, 217, what digits could you place in the ☐? Write to tell how you know.

**5** Do the practice page "Paint by Number."

**6** Copy and complete the chart.

| Number Before | ☺ | Number After |
|---|---|---|
|  | 45,899 |  |
|  | 20,412 |  |
|  | 73,740 |  |
|  | 91,356 |  |
|  | 16,003 |  |

---

**7** Make a list of eight five-digit numbers. Read each number aloud to a friend. Have your pal write each number he hears. Compare the lists.

**8** Use the words to write ten or more five-digit numbers. Write the matching number beside each number word.

| fifty thousand | two hundred |
| forty-eight thousand | eighty |
| nine hundred | sixty-one |

**9** Design a poster to show each place value from ones to ten thousands. Color-code each place value. Then copy five or more numbers from this page. Use the color from the code to draw a line over each digit.

---

**Note to the teacher:** Program the student directions with the number of activities to be completed. Then copy the page and page 10 (back-to-back if desired) for each student.

Name _____

Date _____

# Numbers to 99,999

## Paint by Number

Write the numbers from least to greatest.
Color each number after it is used.

A. _____
B. _____
C. _____
D. _____
E. _____
F. _____
G. _____
H. _____
I. _____
J. _____
K. _____
L. _____

75,024   88,436   52,756   74,183
96,485   10,617   49,315
23,516   32,587   90,237
62,930   49,245

*Choose & Do Math Grids* • ©The Mailbox® Books • TEC61228 • Key p. 90

**Note to the teacher:** Use with page 9.

# Addition and Subtraction Facts

Name _____

Date _____

Choose ___ or more activities to do.
When you finish an activity, color its number.

---

**1** Copy the chart. In each column, write five problems with that sum.

| 10 | 11 | 12 | 13 |
|-----|-----|-----|-----|
| 5 + 5 | | | |
| | | | |

**2** Two numbers can complete this fact family. Write to tell what they are. Write the fact family for each set of three numbers.

### 4

**?**        **9**

**3** Add each number in column A to each number in column B. Write 16 facts.

| A | B |
|---|---|
| 2 | 6 |
| 7 | 3 |
| 4 | 8 |
| 9 | 5 |

---

**4** Draw a picture to show each problem. Solve.

8 + 6 =
15 − 7=
13 − 6 =
9 + 7 =
5 + 8 =

**5** Do the practice page "House of Cards."

**6** Use the numbers in each set to write three different subtraction problems. Solve.

| 14, 5, 8 | 8, 12, 3 | 6, 8, 15 |

14 − 8=
14 − 5=
8 − 5=

---

**7** Share with a friend how a doubles fact can help solve each problem. Then write each sum and show how you used a doubles fact to find it.

6 + 5        8 + 9
5 + 7        7 + 8

**8** Write to tell why 7 + 8 = 15 and 9 + 6 = 15 are not related facts.

**9** Draw a number line for each problem and use it to solve the problem.

11 − 4 =        13 − 8 =        14 − 5 =
15 − 9 =        16 − 9 =        17 − 8 =

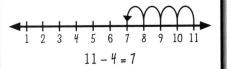

1  2  3  4  5  6  7  8  9  10  11

11 − 4 = 7

---

*Choose & Do Math Grids* • ©The Mailbox® Books • TEC61228 • Key p. 90

# Addition and Subtraction Facts

Name_____     Date_____

## House of Cards

For each large card, find three small cards from below with the matching symbol. Use the numbers to write the fact family.

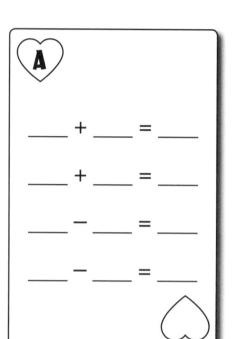

A ♥

___ + ___ = ___

___ + ___ = ___

___ − ___ = ___

___ − ___ = ___

B ♠

___ + ___ = ___

___ − ___ = ___

___ + ___ = ___

___ − ___ = ___

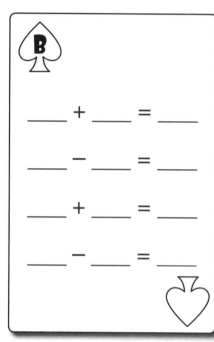

C ♦

___ − ___ = ___

___ − ___ = ___

___ + ___ = ___

___ + ___ = ___

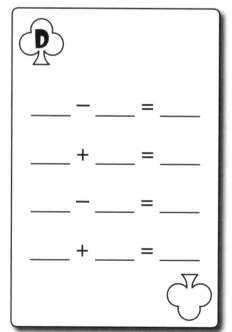

D ♣

___ − ___ = ___

___ + ___ = ___

___ − ___ = ___

___ + ___ = ___

# Two-Digit Addition With One Regrouping

Name _____

Date _____

Choose ___ or more activities to do.
When you finish an activity, color its number.

| | |
|---|---|
| **1** How would you teach another student to solve this problem? Write the steps in order.<br><br>$\begin{array}{r} 35 \\ + 49 \\ \hline \end{array}$ | **2** Copy the problems that have the wrong sums. Solve them.<br><br>$\begin{array}{r} 63 \\ + 27 \\ \hline 80 \end{array}$ $\begin{array}{r} 48 \\ + 17 \\ \hline 65 \end{array}$ $\begin{array}{r} 19 \\ + 35 \\ \hline 44 \end{array}$ $\begin{array}{r} 26 \\ + 58 \\ \hline 74 \end{array}$ |

**3** Write and solve an addition problem for each pair of numbers. Circle the problem that has a sum of 58.

| 25, 57 | 29, 29 | 36, 48 |
|---|---|---|

---

**4** Solve each problem. Use the code.

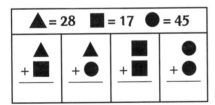

| ▲ = 28 | ■ = 17 | ● = 45 |
|---|---|---|

$\begin{array}{r} ▲ \\ + ■ \\ \hline \end{array}$ $\begin{array}{r} ▲ \\ + ● \\ \hline \end{array}$ $\begin{array}{r} ■ \\ + ■ \\ \hline \end{array}$ $\begin{array}{r} ● \\ + ● \\ \hline \end{array}$

**5** Do the practice page "Make a Splash!"

**6** Write your phone number. Use those numbers to write four or more two-digit addition problems that each use regrouping.

619-555-0047

$\begin{array}{r} \overset{1}{4}7 \\ + \phantom{0}5 \\ \hline 52 \end{array}$

---

**7** Which problem shows regrouping? Tell a partner how you know.

$\begin{array}{r} 56 \\ + 31 \\ \hline \end{array}$ $\begin{array}{r} 75 \\ + 19 \\ \hline \end{array}$ $\begin{array}{r} 34 \\ + 23 \\ \hline \end{array}$

**8** Write and solve five or more addition problems. Use two of the numbers shown in each problem.

| 35 36 37 38 39 |
|---|

**9** Add each number from column B to one of the numbers in column A. Show your work.

| A | B |
|---|---|
| 26 | 38 |
| 15 | 49 |
| 39 | 17 |
| 47 | 25 |

*Choose & Do Math Grids* • ©The Mailbox® Books • TEC61228 • Key p. 90

**Note to the teacher:** Program the student directions with the number of activities to be completed. Then copy the page and page 14 (back-to-back if desired) for each student.

# Two-Digit Addition With One Regrouping

Name_____     Date_____

## Make a Splash!

Add.
Color the water drop with the matching answer.

A.   26
    + 19

B.   36
    + 36

C.   16
    + 57

D.   18
    + 15

E.   29
    + 28

F.   34
    + 29

G.   27
    + 48

H.   27
    + 35

I.   17
    + 54

J.   27
    + 27

K.   24
    + 27

L.   18
    + 54

M.   15
    + 16

N.   45
    + 48

O.   29
    + 62

# ═ Two- and Three-Digit Addition With Regrouping ═

Name _____

Date _____

Choose ____ or more activities to do.
When you finish an activity, color its number.

| | | |
|---|---|---|
| **1** Write and solve ten different addition problems. Use the numbers shown. | **2** Tell what numbers could replace each symbol. | **3** Copy the code. Continue the pattern to Z. Then solve each problem. |

**1** Write and solve ten different addition problems. Use the numbers shown.

26 35 16 49
47 28 29 15

**2** Tell what numbers could replace each symbol.

$$\begin{array}{r} \overset{1\ \ 1}{5\triangle 5} \\ + 33\square \\ \hline \end{array}$$

**3** Copy the code. Continue the pattern to Z. Then solve each problem.

| A = 1, B = 2, C = 3, D = 4 |
|---|

D + Z =          W + H =

P + H =          Z + R =

O + Y =          X + S =

---

**4** Explain why each sum is wrong. Write the correct sums.

$$\begin{array}{r} 326 \\ + 147 \\ \hline 4{,}613 \end{array} \qquad \begin{array}{r} 214 \\ + 393 \\ \hline 5{,}107 \end{array}$$

**5** Do the practice page "Fine-Feathered Fun."

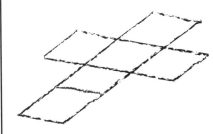

**6** Add the center number to each number on the wheel. You should make six sums.

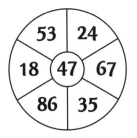

---

**7** Write three addition problems: one with no regrouping, one with one regrouping, and one with two regroupings. Use 462 as the first addend in each problem.

**8** Write each number from 165 to 174. Add each number to itself.

$$\begin{array}{r} \overset{1\ 1}{165} \quad 166 \quad 167 \\ + 165 \\ \hline 330 \end{array}$$

**9** Copy the numbers. Cross out each number that could not be the missing addend. Explain your choices.

$$\begin{array}{r} \overset{1}{33} \\ + \underline{\ \ } \end{array}$$  48    29
                  16    59
                  32    45
                  57    37

*Choose & Do Math Grids* • ©The Mailbox® Books • TEC61228 • Key p. 90

**Note to the teacher:** Program the student directions with the number of activities to be completed. Then copy the page and page 16 (back-to-back if desired) for each student.

# Two- and Three-Digit Addition With Regrouping

Name _____

Date _____

## Fine-Feathered Fun

Add.

| | | | |
|---|---|---|---|
| 266<br>+ 152<br>**T.** | 562<br>+ 363<br>**H.** | 643<br>+ 297<br>**I.** | 174<br>+ 172<br>**O.** |
| 591<br>+ 286<br>**G.** | 426<br>+ 380<br>**S.** | 285<br>+ 135<br>**O.** | 354<br>+ 479<br>**E.** |
| 317<br>+ 384<br>**T.** | 487<br>+ 266<br>**D.** | 732<br>+ 149<br>**L.** | 648<br>+ 237<br>**H.** |
| 507<br>+ 146<br>**T.** | 729<br>+ 258<br>**R.** | 493<br>+ 151<br>**O.** | 155<br>+ 369<br>**E.** |

## Why did the chicken cross the playground?

To solve the riddle, write each letter on its matching numbered line or lines below.

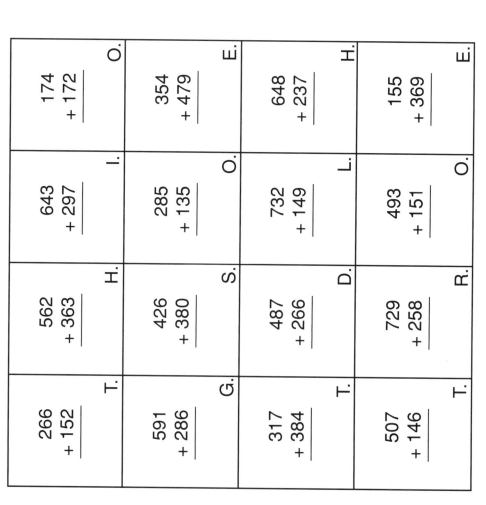

$\overline{653}$ $\overline{346}$ $\overline{877}$ $\overline{524}$ $\overline{418}$ $\overline{701}$ $\overline{644}$

$\overline{653}$ $\overline{925}$ $\overline{833}$ $\overline{420}$ $\overline{701}$ $\overline{885}$ $\overline{524}$ $\overline{987}$

$\overline{806}$ $\overline{881}$ $\overline{940}$ $\overline{753}$ $\overline{833}$ !

*Choose & Do Math Grids* • ©The Mailbox® Books • TEC61228 • Key p. 90

**Note to the teacher:** Use with page 15.

# Two-Digit Subtraction With Regrouping

Name _____

Date _____

Choose ___ or more activities to do.
When you finish an activity, color its number.

| **1** Copy the chart. Subtract the numbers that are next to each other and write the difference in the box below. Then create a subtraction chart of your own. | **2** Write ten pairs of two-digit numbers that would show regrouping when subtracted. | **3** Copy the problem five times. Write a different two-digit number in each one. Solve and show regrouping in each problem. |
|---|---|---|

**1** Copy the chart. Subtract the numbers that are next to each other and write the difference in the box below. Then create a subtraction chart of your own.

| 51 | 25 | 62 | 46 |
|----|----|----|----|

| 26 |
|----|

**2** Write ten pairs of two-digit numbers that would show regrouping when subtracted.

41 and 18
72 and 15

**3** Copy the problem five times. Write a different two-digit number in each one. Solve and show regrouping in each problem.

$$
\begin{array}{r}
50 \\
- \square \\
\hline
\square
\end{array}
$$

**4** Write a letter to a friend. Tell your pal how and why to regroup during subtraction.

**5** Do the practice page "Hoop It Up!"

**6** Find the smallest number. Subtract it from each of the other numbers. Explain your work to a partner.

**54**
**35**
**62**
**29**
**81**

**7** Place the digits 1, 2, 4, 5, 7, and 8 in the problem to make it true.

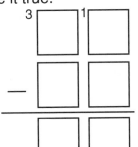

**8** Find three numbers in a row or column that can be used to complete the number sentence below.

| 52 | 63 | 95 |
|----|----|----|
| 14 | 17 | 38 |
| 48 | 21 | 57 |

$\square - \square = \square$

**9** Pretend you are solving each problem with base ten blocks. Draw a model to show each difference.

$$
\begin{array}{r} 94 \\ -25 \\ \hline \end{array}
\qquad
\begin{array}{r} 53 \\ -18 \\ \hline \end{array}
\qquad
\begin{array}{r} 74 \\ -57 \\ \hline \end{array}
$$

*Choose & Do Math Grids* • ©The Mailbox® Books • TEC61228 • Key p. 91

**Note to the teacher:** Program the student directions with the number of activities to be completed. Then copy the page and page 18 (back-to-back if desired) for each student.

# Two-Digit Subtraction With Regrouping

Name_____ Date _____

## Hoop It Up!

Check each problem.
If the answer is correct, color the basketball orange.
If the answer is incorrect, write the correct difference.

A.  51
  − 14
  ‾‾‾‾
    47

B.  98
  − 19
  ‾‾‾‾
    89

C.  37
  − 18
  ‾‾‾‾
    19

D.  62
  − 19
  ‾‾‾‾
    43

E.  47
  − 29
  ‾‾‾‾
    28

F.  90
  − 24
  ‾‾‾‾
    66

G.  53
  − 47
  ‾‾‾‾
     6

H.  76
  − 38
  ‾‾‾‾
    48

I.  22
  − 13
  ‾‾‾‾
     9

J.  30
  − 13
  ‾‾‾‾
    17

K.  93
  − 34
  ‾‾‾‾
    59

L.  62
  − 19
  ‾‾‾‾
    57

Each orange ball is worth two points.
How many points were scored? _____

*Choose & Do Math Grids* • ©The Mailbox® Books • TEC61228 • Key p. 91

**Note to the teacher:** Use with page 17.

# Two- and Three-Digit Subtraction With Regrouping

Name _____

Date _____

Choose ___ or more activities to do.
When you finish an activity, color its number.

| **1** Choose the number that fits the problem. Tell why the other numbers won't work. | **2** For each set, write the largest three-digit number you can make. Then write the smallest three-digit number you can make. Subtract. | **3** Without subtracting, choose the problem that needs regrouping. Explain your choice to a partner. |
|---|---|---|
| 4 13<br>5̶3̶4<br>−☐☐☐    651<br>162<br>203<br>318 | 4, 8, 1   8, 3, 9   3, 2, 7<br>5, 7, 4    5, 2, 6 | 627     586<br>− 253    − 271 |
| **4** Subtract the smallest number from each of the other numbers. | **5** Do the practice page "Meet the Champ." | **6** Subtract each number in column B from a different number in column A. Show your work. |
| 810   723   541<br>302   631   287<br>456   702   365 |  | **A**     **B**<br>853    347<br>765    419<br>634    281<br>512    176<br>740    395 |
| **7** Write a subtraction word problem using three-digit numbers. Make sure the problem needs regrouping. | **8** List ten three-digit numbers to subtract from 403. If the problem would need regrouping, circle the number. | **9** Write and solve eight subtraction problems that each use three-digit numbers. Then use addition to check your work. |
|  | 403<br>−☐☐☐    201<br>(365)<br>(129)  |  |

*Choose & Do Math Grids* • ©The Mailbox® Books • TEC61228 • Key p. 91

**Note to the teacher:** Program the student directions with the number of activities to be completed. Then copy the page and page 20 (back-to-back if desired) for each student.

# Two- and Three-Digit Subtraction With Regrouping

Name _____

Date _____

## Meet the Champ

Use the numbers on each trophy to write three different subtraction problems.

Solve each problem.

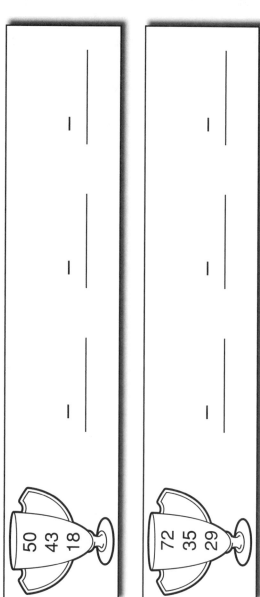

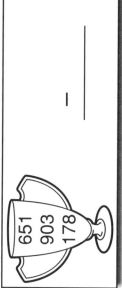

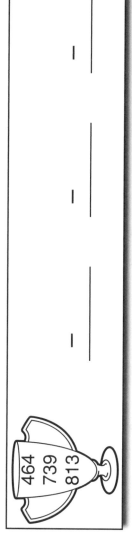

50
43
18

72
35
29

464
739
813

651
903
178

*Choose & Do Math Grids* • ©The Mailbox® Books • TEC61228 • Key p. 91

**Note to the teacher:** Use with page 19.

# Addition and Subtraction
## Two digits without regrouping

Name _____

Date _____

Choose ____ or more activities to do.
When you finish an activity, color its number.

| | | |
|---|---|---|
| **1** Use the numbers shown. Write and solve eight addition problems. | **2** Use only two-digit doubles. Write and solve eight problems with sums of 99 or less. Make sure each answer is a double. | **3** Write and solve four addition problems and four subtraction problems. Each problem should equal 64. Use two-digit numbers. |
| | $$\begin{array}{r} 55 \\ + 11 \\ \hline 66 \end{array}$$ | $$\begin{array}{r} 31 \\ + 33 \\ \hline 64 \end{array} \qquad \begin{array}{r} 96 \\ - 32 \\ \hline 64 \end{array}$$ |
| **4** Use the code. Draw a picture of each problem and its answer. | **5** Do the practice page "Nuts About Peanuts." | **6** Make a poster. Show how to subtract a two-digit number from another two-digit number. Use different colors and arrows. |
| ten = 10   one = ⬭ |  | |
| $$\begin{array}{r} 27 \\ + 51 \\ \hline \end{array} \qquad \begin{array}{r} 43 \\ - 42 \\ \hline \end{array}$$ | | |
| **7** Write the steps you would take to find the difference of these two numbers. Read the steps to a friend and have your pal follow them.   45    32 | **8** Decide what number each symbol stands for. Write and solve the problems. $$\begin{array}{r} \triangle \; \triangle \\ + \triangle \; \heartsuit \\ \hline 6 \quad 5 \end{array} \qquad \begin{array}{r} \florette\;\florette \\ + \heartsuit\;\florette \\ \hline 6 \quad 8 \end{array}$$ | **9** Copy and correct each problem. Write to explain the mistake that was made each time. $$\begin{array}{r} 87 \\ - 53 \\ \hline 44 \end{array} \qquad \begin{array}{r} 38 \\ - 15 \\ \hline 24 \end{array}$$ |

In box 1:
| | 32 | |
|---|---|---|
| 21 | 65 | 14 |
| | 33 | |

*Choose & Do Math Grids* • ©The Mailbox® Books • TEC61228 • Key p. 91

---

**Note to the teacher:** Program the student directions with the number of activities to be completed. Then copy the page and page 22 (back-to-back if desired) for each student.

# Addition and Subtraction

Two digits without regrouping

Name______________________________ Date____________________

## Nuts About Peanuts

Add or subtract.
Circle the answer in the puzzle.

**Peanuts**

| | | | | |
|---|---|---|---|---|
| 9 | 8 | 4 | 8 | 3 |
| 9 | 5 | 6 | 1 | 2 |
| 2 | 0 | 9 | 7 | 4 |
| 6 | 3 | 5 | 4 | 9 |

A. $58 - 26$

B. $81 + 16$

C. $68 - 20$

D. $24 - 12$

E. $98 - 14$

F. $13 + 33$

G. $40 + 14$

H. $75 - 14$

I. $11 + 72$

J. $42 + 56$

K. $89 - 26$

L. $60 + 39$

M. $51 + 34$

N. $15 + 80$

O. $47 - 30$

P. $72 - 52$

Q. $43 + 31$

R. $71 - 21$

S. $38 + 11$



 **Note to the teacher:** Use with page 21.

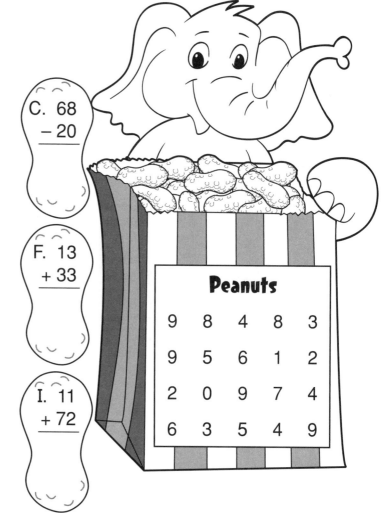

# Addition and Subtraction
## Two digits with regrouping

Name _____

Date _____

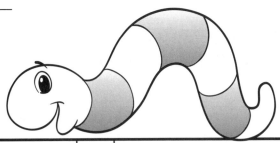

Choose ___ or more activities to do.
When you finish an activity, color its number.

| **1** Cut a stop-sign shape. On one side, write how you know to regroup when adding. On the other side, write how you know to regroup when subtracting.  | **2** Write five problems, each with a sum or difference of 55. Use two-digit numbers in each problem and be sure to regroup in each problem. | **3** Copy the chart. For each problem, write a number that makes the problem true. |
|---|---|---|

For activity 3:

| 63 − ___ 39 | 92 − ___ 39 | 71 − ___ 39 |
|---|---|---|
| 78 − ___ 39 | 80 − ___ 39 | 55 − ___ 39 |

| **4** Copy the puzzle. Write a number in each circle. When you add the two circles on each side, you should get the sum found in the rectangle. 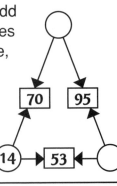 | **5** Do the practice page "Crunching Numbers."  | **6** Copy the chart. Start at 62. Follow the arrows. Add or subtract. 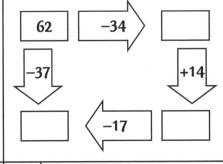 |
|---|---|---|

| **7** Check this problem.  $72 - 18 = 66$  Is the answer correct? If not, what is the correct answer? Write to explain two ways you can check the answer to a subtraction problem. | **8** Choose two numbers from below. Use them to write and solve an addition or a subtraction problem. Repeat. Make eight different problems in all.  17  59   28  33   71    45 | **9** Write steps or draw pictures to show how to solve each problem. Use your work to teach a friend.  46      62  − 28    + 29 |
|---|---|---|

**Note to the teacher:** Program the student directions with the number of activities to be completed. Then copy the page and page 24 (back-to-back if desired) for each student.

# Addition and Subtraction
## Two digits with regrouping

Name _____    Date _____

## Crunching Numbers

Add or subtract.
Color the apple with the matching answer.

| | | | |
|---|---|---|---|
| A.    63<br>    − 18 | B.    47<br>    + 24 | C.    87<br>    − 38 | D.    54<br>    − 29 |

A.    63
    − 18

B.    47
    + 24

C.    87
    − 38

D.    54
    − 29

E.    59
    + 28

F.    25
    + 39

G.    32
    − 14

H.    55
    + 36

I.    65
    + 17

J.    64
    − 47

K.    72
    − 46

L.    11
    + 19

M.    90
    − 53

N.    85
    − 38

O.    13
    + 57

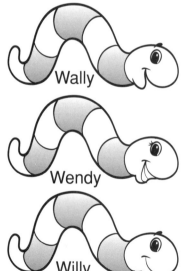

Wally

Wendy

Willy

| 25 | 91 | 30 | 37 | 33 | 28 |
|----|----|----|----|----|----|
| 45 | 71 | 49 | 17 | 26 | 31 |
| 87 | 64 | 18 | 82 | 47 | 70 |

The winner of the apple-eating contest is the worm with the most apples colored.

The winner is _____.

# Addition and Subtraction
## Two and three digits without regrouping

Name _____

Date _____

Choose ____ or more activities to do.
When you finish an activity, color its number.

---

**1** | Use the numbers to write and solve five addition problems. Then write and solve five subtraction problems.

| 10 | 20 | 21 | 22 | 23 | 24 | 30 | 31 |
|----|----|----|----|----|----|----|----|
| 32 | 33 | 34 | 40 | 41 | 42 | 43 | 44 |

**2** | Solve the riddle.

> **I am a two-digit number. When you add me to myself, you get a sum of 24. What number am I?**

Write to tell how you solved the riddle.

**3** | Write your zip code. Use the digits to make two-digit numbers. Find how many addition and subtraction problems (without regrouping) you can make with the numbers. Write and solve each problem.

> 27403
> 27 + 40 = 67    47 − 20 = 27

---

**4** | Copy and complete the chart.

|      | Add 122. | Subtract 122. |
|------|----------|---------------|
| 375  |          |               |
| 756  |          |               |
| 562  |          |               |
| 624  |          |               |
| 243  |          |               |

**5** | Do the practice page "Learn the Steps."

Dance Like a Star

**6** | Copy and complete the chart.

| | |
|---|---|
| A. | 57¢ − ☐ = 25¢ |
| B. | ☐ + 40¢ = 65¢ |
| C. | ☐ + 54¢ = 78¢ |
| D. | 86¢ − ☐ = 73¢ |
| E. | ☐ + 86¢ = 96¢ |
| F. | 99¢ − ☐ = 38¢ |

---

**7** | Work with a partner. Take turns rolling two or three dice. Write each player's numbers. Use the numbers to write an addition or a subtraction problem that does not use regrouping. Make and solve ten problems.

**8** | Copy each answer. Write a matching problem. Use two- and three-digit numbers.

| + 657 | − 503 |
|-------|-------|
| + 441 | + 982 |

**9** | Draw a picture to solve each problem. Write to explain a faster way to solve each problem.

$$\begin{array}{r} 261 \\ + 138 \\ \hline \end{array} \qquad \begin{array}{r} 352 \\ - 201 \\ \hline \end{array}$$

---

*Choose & Do Math Grids* • ©The Mailbox® Books • TEC61228 • Key p. 91

**Note to the teacher:** Provide access to two or three dice to complete activity 7. Program the student directions with the number of activities to be completed. Then copy the page and page 26 (back-to-back if desired) for each student.

# Addition and Subtraction

## Two and three digits without regrouping

Name_____ Date_____

## Learn the Steps

Add or subtract.

| | | |
|---|---|---|
| 59<br>− 43<br><br>A | 197<br>− 151<br><br>E | 38<br>+ 51<br><br>O |
| 659<br>− 546<br><br>Y | 205<br>+ 263<br><br>F | 48<br>− 20<br><br>H |
| 333<br>− 231<br><br>L | 76<br>+ 22<br><br>T | |
| 65<br>− 24<br><br>V | 418<br>+ 110<br><br>W | |

**Why don't dogs make good dancers?**
To solve the riddle, write each letter from above on the
matching numbered line or lines below.

‾98‾ ‾28‾ ‾46‾ ‾113‾   ‾28‾ ‾16‾ ‾41‾ ‾46‾   ‾98‾ ‾528‾ ‾89‾   ‾102‾ ‾46‾ ‾468‾ ‾98‾   ‾468‾ ‾46‾ ‾46‾ ‾98‾ .

*Choose & Do Math Grids* • ©The Mailbox® Books • TEC61228 • Key p. 91

# Addition and Subtraction
## Two and three digits with regrouping

Name _____

Date _____

Choose ___ or more activities to do.
When you finish an activity, color its number.

| **1** Copy and complete each chart. | **2** Add the number on the left to each number on the right. Then subtract each number on the right from the number on the left. | **3** Draw a six-section spinner. Write a two- or three-digit number in each space. Use a paper clip and a pencil to spin twice. Write the numbers in an addition problem and a subtraction problem. Solve. Repeat four more times. |
|---|---|---|

**1** Copy and complete each chart.

| Add 126. | | Subtract 78. | |
|---|---|---|---|
| 57 | | 90 | |
| 84 | | 165 | |
| 415 | | 353 | |
| 780 | | 502 | |

**2** Add the number on the left to each number on the right. Then subtract each number on the right from the number on the left.

$1.95

$1.18
$1.27
$1.49
$1.66

**3** Draw a six-section spinner. Write a two- or three-digit number in each space. Use a paper clip and a pencil to spin twice. Write the numbers in an addition problem and a subtraction problem. Solve. Repeat four more times.

---

**4** Write 250 on your paper. Subtract one of the numbers shown. Then subtract another number shown from the answer. Repeat until you have an answer of 100 or less.

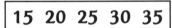

| 15 | 20 | 25 | 30 | 35 |

**5** Do the practice page "Bowling Night."

**6** Copy and solve each problem. Write to tell how the problems are alike and different.

819        554
− 265      + 265

---

**7** Copy the problem. Use one strategy to subtract. Then write or draw to show another way you could solve the problem. Explain how to check your answer.

720
− 265

**8** Cut a sheet of paper to make six cards. Label each card with a different digit (1–9). Put the cards in two rows. Add the three-digit numbers. Switch two cards and repeat. Make and solve six different problems.

**9** If 300 + 🎳 = 450 and 560 − 🎳 = 410, what is the value of 🎳? Write two more problems where 🎳 has the same value.

**Note to the teacher:** Program the student directions with the number of activities to be completed. Then copy the page and page 28 (back-to-back if desired) for each student.

Name _____

Date _____

# Addition and Subtraction
## Two and three digits with regrouping

## Bowling Night

Use the table to write the scores.
Add or subtract.

| Final Scores | |
|---|---|
| Bailey | 132 |
| Bea | 57 |
| Bill | 148 |
| Bob | 119 |
| Bonnie | 157 |
| Buster | 106 |

**A.**
Buster's score
Bea's score
+ _____

**B.**
Bob's score
Bea's score
+ _____

**C.**
Bonnie's score
Bill's score
− _____

**D.**
Bailey's score
Bob's score
+ _____

**E.**
Buster's score
Bea's score
− _____

**F.**
Bailey's score
Buster's score
− _____

**G.**
Bill's score
Bob's score
− _____

**H.**
Bonnie's score
Bill's score
+ _____

**Note to the teacher:** Use with page 27.

# Multiplication Facts (0-5)

Name _____

Date _____

Choose ___ or more activities to do.
When you finish an activity, color its number.

---

**1** | Color nine arrays on graph paper. Show each multiplication fact from 4 x 1 to 4 x 9.

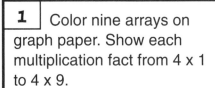

4 x 2 = 8

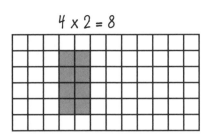

---

**2** | Draw pictures to show that each pair of facts has the same product.

| 2 x 3<br>3 x 2 | 1 x 5<br>5 x 1 |
|---|---|
| 3 x 4<br>4 x 3 | 4 x 2<br>2 x 4 |

---

**3** | Copy and complete the problems. Then write a rule for multiplying by 1.

0 x 1 = ___       ___ x 1 = 1

2 x ___ = 2       ___ x 1 = 3

4 x 1 = ___       5 x ___ = 5

---

**4** | How can skip-counting help you solve a multiplication problem? List your ideas and then share them with a friend.

---

**5** | Do the practice page "Exactly Even."

---

**6** | Order the words to tell the zero property. Write the sentence.

| number | Any |
|---|---|
| multiplied | equals |
| zero     zero. | by |

Write five facts that prove this property.

---

**7** | Copy and complete the table.

| x | 0 | 1 | 2 | 3 | 4 | 5 |
|---|---|---|---|---|---|---|
| 0 | | | | | | |
| 1 | | | | | | |
| 2 | | | | | | |
| 3 | | | | | | |
| 4 | | | | | | |
| 5 | | | | | | |

---

**8** | Write three or more ways to find the total number of fingers.

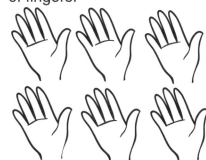

---

**9** | Write 16 facts. Multiply each number in column A by each number in column B.

| A | B |
|---|---|
| 2 | 6 |
| 3 | 7 |
| 4 | 8 |
| 5 | 9 |

---

*Choose & Do Math Grids* • ©The Mailbox® Books • TEC61228 • Key p. 92

**Note to the teacher:** Program the student directions with the number of activities to be completed. Then copy the page and page 30 (back-to-back if desired) for each student.

29

# Multiplication Facts (0-5)

## Exactly Even

Write two problems from the box
  on each balance scale.
Mark off the problems in the box.

| 2 x 3 | 4 x 6 | 2 x 8 | 0 x 7 | 1 x 9 | 4 x 1 | 2 x 9 | 3 x 8 |
| 3 x 4 | 3 x 3 | 3 x 6 | 2 x 2 | 2 x 6 | 4 x 4 | 1 x 6 | 5 x 0 |

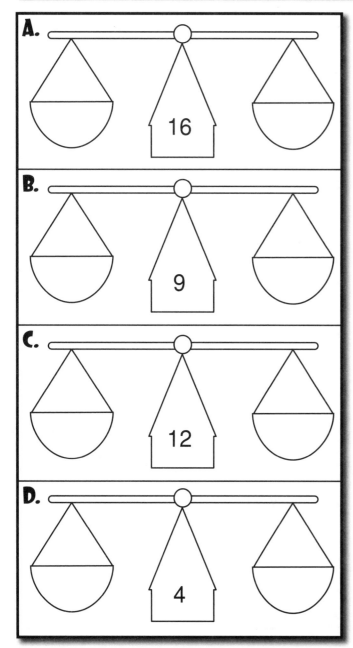

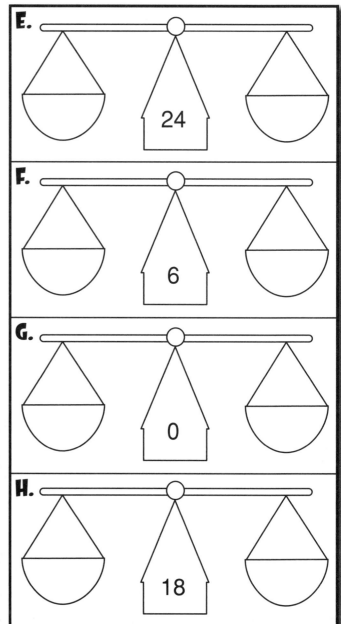

*Choose & Do Math Grids* • ©The Mailbox® Books • TEC61228 • Key p. 92

# Multiplication Facts (6-9)

Name _____

Date _____

Choose ____ or more activities to do.
When you finish an activity, color its number.

---

**1** Copy the spinners. Use a pencil and paper clip to spin each one. Write a multiplication sentence using the numbers spun. Repeat ten or more times.

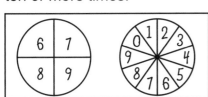

**2** Use the code to write ten different multiplication facts.

$\square$ = 6     $\square$ = 8

$\boxtimes$ = 7     $\square$ = 9

$\boxtimes$ x $\square$ = 56

**3** Rewrite each addition problem as a multiplication fact.

A. 7 + 7 + 7 =
B. 9 + 9 =
C. 6 + 6 + 6 + 6 + 6 =
D. 9 + 9 + 9 =
E. 8 + 8 + 8 + 8 =
F. 7 + 7 + 7 + 7 =

---

**4** Copy and complete the table.

| x | 6 | 9 | 8 | 7 |
|---|---|---|---|---|
| 7 | 42 |   |   |   |
| 9 |   |   | 72 |   |
| 4 |   |   |   |   |
| 8 |   | 72 |   |   |

**5** Do the practice page "Leaky Pipes."

**6** Find the value of each symbol.

6 x 9 = △●     7 x 7 = ●□
8 x 7 = △■     8 x 8 = ■●
9 x 3 = ▲○     9 x 8 = ○▲

---

**7** Write all the nines facts in order from 9 x 1 through 9 x 9. Write about the patterns you see.

**8** Make a trail game to practice your multiplication facts for numbers 6 through 9. Play the game with a friend.

**9** Copy and complete the tables. Write a rule for each table.

| 7 | 49 |
|---|---|
| 5 | 35 |
| 6 |   |
|   | 21 |
| 9 |   |

| 6 | 54 |
|---|---|
| 3 | 27 |
|   | 72 |
| 4 |   |
|   | 81 |

---

*Choose & Do Math Grids* • ©The Mailbox® Books • TEC61228 • Key p. 92

# Multiplication Facts (6-9)

Name_____    Date_____

## Leaky Pipes

Multiply.
Cross out the matching product in a puddle.

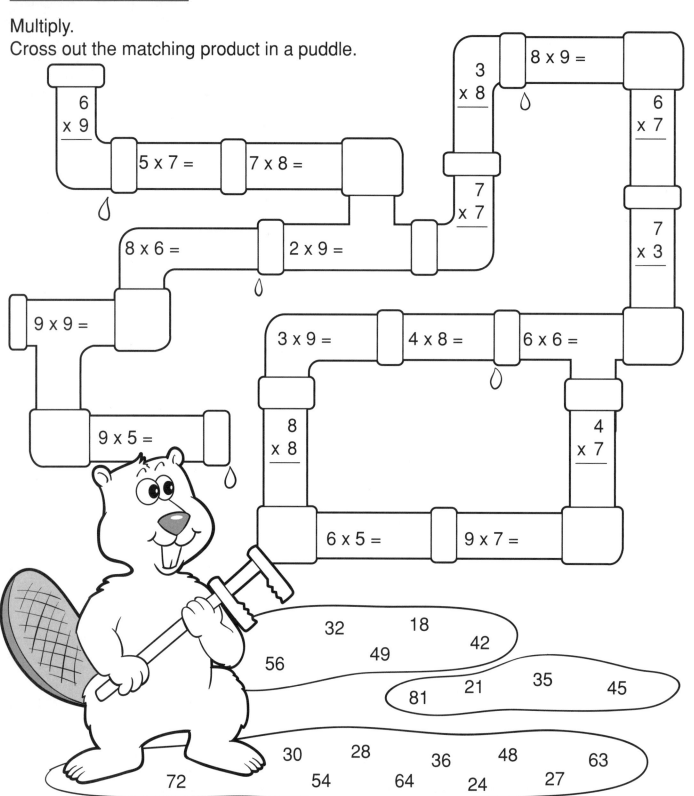

# Multiplying Two Digits by One Digit

Name _____

Date _____

Choose ___ or more activities to do.
When you finish an activity, color its number.

---

**1** | Look at the problem. Explain to a partner why the answer is wrong.

$$\begin{array}{r} 56 \\ \times\ 3 \\ \hline 158 \end{array}$$

---

**2** | Copy and solve. Use the code.

1○        △1        ○○
x △        x □        x □
___        ___        ___

| **Code** |
| △ = 2   □ = 3   ○ = 4 |

---

**3** | Solve each problem. Then multiply each product by 3.

$$\begin{array}{r} 47 \\ \times\ 2 \\ \hline \end{array} \quad \begin{array}{r} 28 \\ \times\ 3 \\ \hline \end{array} \quad \begin{array}{r} 19 \\ \times\ 4 \\ \hline \end{array}$$

---

**4** | This model shows lattice multiplication. Study it. Then use the same method to solve five problems of your own.

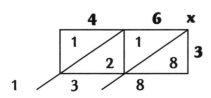

---

**5** | Do the practice page "Times Tables."

---

**6** | Write and solve a multiplication problem for each pair of numbers. Circle the problems that have the same product.

A. 68, 3
B. 5, 37
C. 8, 43
D. 86, 4

---

**7** | Fill in the blanks to make the number sentence true. Then show four more pairs of numbers that make the sentence true.

____ x ____ = 144

---

**8** | For each set of digits, write and solve three two-digit by one-digit multiplication problems.

| 2, 4, 6 | 3, 4, 8 |
| 1, 5, 6 | |

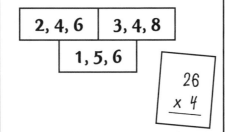

$$\begin{array}{r} 26 \\ \times\ 4 \\ \hline \end{array}$$

---

**9** | Write >, <, or = in each circle. Then create a multi-digit multiplication sentence of your own for each symbol.

| 2 x 21 ○ 4 x 11 |
| 3 x 43 ○ 4 x 32 |
| 3 x 15 ○ 2 x 48 |

---

*Choose & Do Math Grids* • ©The Mailbox® Books • TEC61228 • Key p. 92

**Note to the teacher:** Program the student directions with the number of activities to be completed. Then copy the page and page 34 (back-to-back if desired) for each student.

# Multiplying Two Digits by One Digit

Name_____     Date_____

## Times Tables

On each table, write a multiplication problem
   using the numbers shown.
Multiply.
Cross out the product on the menu.

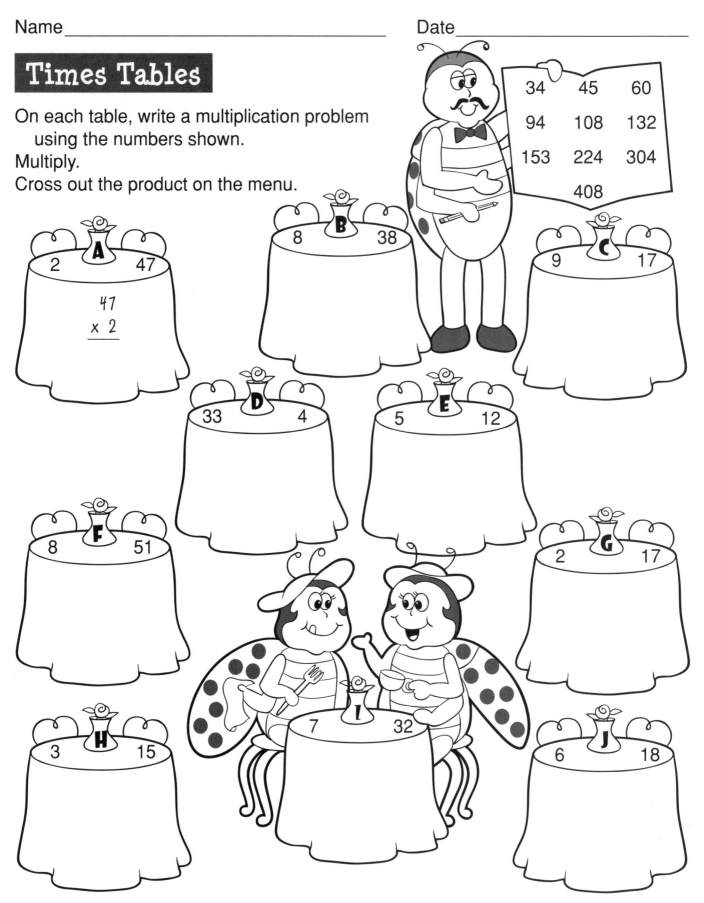

| 34 | 45 | 60 |
|----|----|----|
| 94 | 108 | 132 |
| 153 | 224 | 304 |
|  | 408 |  |

**A** 2    47

$$\begin{array}{r} 47 \\ \times\ 2 \\ \hline \end{array}$$

**B** 8    38

**C** 9    17

**D** 33    4

**E** 5    12

**F** 8    51

**G** 2    17

**H** 3    15

**I** 7    32

**J** 6    18

# Division Facts (0-5 as Divisors)

Name _____

Date _____

Choose ___ or more activities to do.
When you finish an activity, color its number.

| | |
|---|---|

**1** Draw a flower garden with 24 flowers. Circle three equal groups. Write a division fact to go with your picture. Repeat with 4, 6, and 8 groups.

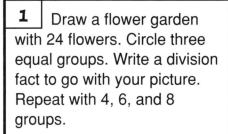

**2** Explain what is wrong with this problem.

$$4 \div 0 = 0$$

**3** Roll a die. If the number rolled can be evenly divided into a number on the grid, write the division sentence. Keep rolling until every number has been used.

| 30 | 8 | 9 | 15 |
|----|----|----|----|
| 24 | 18 | 12 | 20 |

**4** Copy and fill in the blanks.

- When a number is divided by 1, the answer will be _____.

- When a number is divided by itself, the answer will be _____.

Give five examples for each rule.

**5** Do the practice page "Going on a Picnic."

**6** What number or numbers can go in the box? Explain.

$$0 \div \square = 0$$

**7** Divide your paper into four sections. Draw 12 eggs in each section. Show four different ways to equally group each set of eggs.

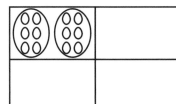

**8** Make three charts. Show how to divide by 2, 3, and 4. Include at least six numbers in each column.

| ÷ 2 | |
|-----|-----|
| 14 | 7 |
| 10 | 5 |
| 8 | 4 |

**9** Draw number lines to show each problem.

$10 \div 5 =$  $\quad$  $14 \div 2 =$

$16 \div 4 =$  $\quad$  $12 \div 3 =$

$6 \div 2 =$  $\quad$  $15 \div 5 =$

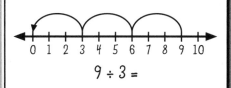

$9 \div 3 =$

*Choose & Do Math Grids* • ©The Mailbox® Books • TEC61228 • Key p. 92

**Note to the teacher:** For activity 3, prepare a die by covering the 6 face with a piece of masking tape. Then draw two dots on the masking tape. Program the student directions with the number of activities to be completed. Then copy the page and page 36 (back-to-back if desired) for each student.

# Division Facts (0-5 as Divisors)

Name_____  Date_____

## Going on a Picnic

Divide. Write each item on the basket with the matching quotient.

| Picnic List | |
|---|---|
| watermelon | $4 \div 2 =$ ___ |
| apple | $16 \div 4 =$ ___ |
| banana | $5 \div 5 =$ ___ |
| pear | $3 \div 1 =$ ___ |
| grapes | $10 \div 2 =$ ___ |
| soda | $12 \div 4 =$ ___ |
| iced tea | $25 \div 5 =$ ___ |
| lemonade | $8 \div 2 =$ ___ |
| water | $10 \div 5 =$ ___ |
| juice | $3 \div 3 =$ ___ |
| sandwich | $4 \div 1 =$ ___ |
| chicken | $6 \div 3 =$ ___ |
| salad | $15 \div 3 =$ ___ |
| wrap | $1 \div 1 =$ ___ |
| bagel | $9 \div 3 =$ ___ |
| cookie | $2 \div 2 =$ ___ |
| chips | $8 \div 4 =$ ___ |
| cupcake | $6 \div 2 =$ ___ |
| brownie | $20 \div 4 =$ ___ |
| doughnut | $12 \div 3 =$ ___ |

Choose & Do Math Grids • ©The Mailbox® Books • TEC61228 • Key p. 92

# Division Facts Through Nine

Name _____

Date _____

Choose ___ or more activities to do.
When you finish an activity, color its number.

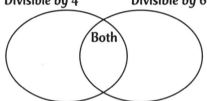
dividend ÷ divisor = quotient

| **1** For each number, write three different division problems. Start each problem with the number. | **2** Copy the numbers. Write a division problem for each number that can be divided evenly by seven. | **3** Copy the Venn diagram. Write each number in the matching section. |
|---|---|---|
| 12  16  18  24  36 $$12 \div 2 = 6$$ $$12 \div 1 = 12$$ $$12 \div 3 = 4$$ | 24  21  49  43  63  42  56 14  36  7  35  52  61  28 | **Evenly Divisible by 4**   **Evenly Divisible by 6**  Both  6, 12, 16, 18, 20, 24, 28, 30, 32, 36, 42 |
| **4** Write a different division problem on each of 12 cards. Write the matching quotients on 12 more cards. Use the cards to play a memory game.   | **5** Do the practice page "Snacktime."  | **6** Copy the numbers. For each set, cross out the number that does not belong. Write a division fact for the uncrossed numbers. |
| | | \| 7, 6, 45, 42 \| 36, 9, 4, 3 \| 4, 5, 32, 8 \| 56, 54, 9, 6 \| |
| **7** Write six or more division facts. Check each answer using repeated subtraction. $$9 \div 3 = 3$$ 9 – 3 = 6   6 – 3 = 3   3 – 3 = 0     1             2             3 | **8** Make a division quiz that has ten problems. Also make an answer key. Ask a classmate to take the quiz. Use the key to check the answers. | **9** Write about a time you might use division in your life. Use numbers in your example. *I might use division if my mom bakes cookies. If she bakes 24 cookies, and there are 4 people in my family, I might want to know how many cookies each person can have if each person gets the same number of cookies.* |

*Choose & Do Math Grids* • ©The Mailbox® Books • TEC61228 • Key p. 92

**Note to the teacher:** Program the student directions with the number of activities to be completed. Then copy the page and page 38 (back-to-back if desired) for each student.

# Division Facts Through Nine

Name_____  Date_____

## Snacktime

Divide.
Cross out the incorrect quotient.

| | | |
|---|---|---|
| 30 ÷ 6 = | 4 S | 5 T |
| 49 ÷ 7 = | 7 H | 8 N |
| 27 ÷ 9 = | 2 F | 3 E |
| 72 ÷ 9 = | 8 Y | 9 B |
| 54 ÷ 6 = | 8 C | 9 A |
| 42 ÷ 7 = | 6 R | 7 K |
| 35 ÷ 5 = | 7 E | 8 J |
| 64 ÷ 8 = | 8 S | 9 W |
| 36 ÷ 6 = | 5 H | 6 M |
| 45 ÷ 5 = | 8 O | 9 A |
| 48 ÷ 8 = | 5 K | 6 R |
| 18 ÷ 9 = | 2 T | 3 L |
| 28 ÷ 7 = | 4 K | 5 F |
| 24 ÷ 4 = | 6 I | 7 E |
| 56 ÷ 8 = | 7 D | 8 C |
| 16 ÷ 4 = | 3 Q | 4 S |

**Why do baby goats know how to divide?**
To solve the riddle, write each unmarked letter from the chart in order on the lines below.

— — — —   — — —

— — — —   — — — — !

# ═ Multiplication and Division Facts Through Nine ═

Name _____

Date _____

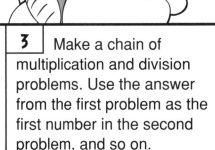

Choose ____ or more activities to do.
When you finish an activity, color its number.

| **1** Copy and solve each problem. Write a multiplication fact that can help you check each answer. | **2** Use two numbers from each set to write a multiplication story problem and a division story problem. The answer for each problem should be the third number. | **3** Make a chain of multiplication and division problems. Use the answer from the first problem as the first number in the second problem, and so on. |
|---|---|---|

**1**

A. $63 \div 7 =$    B. $56 \div 8 =$
C. $42 \div 6 =$    D. $27 \div 3 =$
E. $32 \div 4 =$    F. $45 \div 5 =$

**2**

| 4, 7, 28 | 6, 9, 54 | 5, 8, 40 |
|---|---|---|

**3**

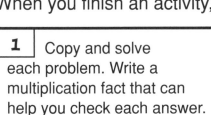

$9 \times 4 = 36$
$36 \div 6 = 6$
$6 \times 2 = 12$

---

| **4** Make a list of ten multiplication facts. Read each problem to a partner. Have your partner say the product and then name a related division fact. Switch roles. | **5** Do the practice page "Fearless!" | **6** Sort the numbers into four sets of three. Create a multiplication and division fact family for each set of numbers. |
|---|---|---|

**5**

**6**

| 2 | 3 | 4 | 5 |
|---|---|---|---|
| 5 | 7 | 8 | 9 |
| 18 | 20 | 24 | 35 |

---

| **7** Write to tell how the meanings of *product* and *quotient* are alike. Write to tell how they are different. | **8** Copy each number set. Write the missing symbol or number. | **9** Make ten or more triangle-shaped flash cards. Use the cards to practice your multiplication and division facts. |
|---|---|---|

**8**

| 4   7 = 28 | 36   6 = 6 | 8 x   = 64 |
|---|---|---|
| 72 ÷ 9 = |   x 6 = 30 | 9   4 = 36 |
| 9 x   = 81 | 25 ÷   = 5 | 3 x   = 12 |
|   ÷ 2 = 7 | 3 x   = 24 | 6   6 = 1 |

**9**

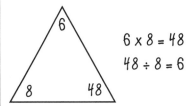

$6 \times 8 = 48$
$48 \div 8 = 6$

---

*Choose & Do Math Grids* • ©The Mailbox® Books • TEC61228 • Key p. 92

**Note to the teacher:** Program the student directions with the number of activities to be completed. Then copy the page and page 40 (back-to-back if desired) for each student.

39

# = Multiplication and Division Facts Through Nine =

Name_____ Date_____

## Fearless!

Write the missing number in each problem.
Write the number in the puzzle.

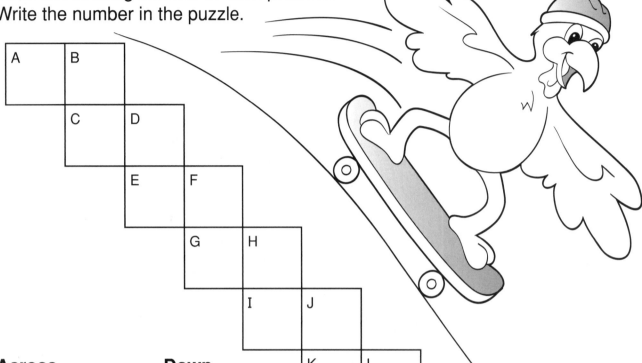

**Across**

A. $2 \times 6 =$ ____

C. $8 \times 5 =$ ____

E. $6 \times 6 =$ ____

G. $5 \times 9 =$ ____

I.  $6 \times 8 =$ ____

K. $4 \times 4 =$ ____

M. $5 \times 6 =$ ____

O. $8 \times 9 =$ ____

Q. $2 \times 1 =$ ____

S. $7 \times 6 =$ ____

**Down**

B. ____ $\div 4 = 6$

D. $9 \div 3 =$ ____

F. ____ $\div 8 = 8$

H. ____ $\div 6 = 9$

J. ____ $\div 9 = 9$

L. ____ $\div 9 = 7$

N. $7 \div 1 =$ ____

P. ____ $\div 5 = 4$

R. ____ $\div 3 = 8$

T. ____ $\div 9 = 3$

# ═ Multiplication and Division of Larger Numbers ═

Name _____

Date _____

Choose ____ or more activities to do.
When you finish an activity, color its number.

---

**1** Draw the wheel. In each section, write a number greater than 50 that can be equally divided by 5. Check your work.

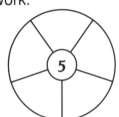

**2** Copy and solve each problem. Write the steps to solve the problems. Tell how each product is alike and why.

| 21 | 31 | 41 |
|---|---|---|
| x 8 | x 8 | x 8 |

| 51 | 61 | 71 |
|---|---|---|
| x 8 | x 8 | x 8 |

**3** What is a remainder? Which problem will have a remainder? Explain how you know.

$$2\overline{)87} \qquad 2\overline{)78}$$

---

**4** Copy and correct each problem. Explain each mistake that was made.

| $\overset{1}{15}$ | 47 | $\overset{2}{26}$ | 204 |
|---|---|---|---|
| x 5 | 3$\overline{)144}$ | x 4 | 5$\overline{)120}$ |
| 60 | -12 | 164 | -10 |
| | 24 | | 2 |
| | -24 | | -0 |
| | 0 | | 20 |

**5** Do the practice page "Stocking Up."

**6** Copy each problem. Circle each one you can solve in your head. Write the product.

| 30 x 2 = | 78 x 6 = | 51 x 4 = |
|---|---|---|
| 29 x 9 = | 15 x 3 = | 47 x 5 = |
| 62 x 3 = | 80 x 2 = | 93 x 7 = |

---

**7** Find each answer.

| 42 | |
|---|---|
| x 4 | 4$\overline{)168}$ |

Make a T chart. List ways the steps are the same and ways they are different.

| Alike | Different |
|---|---|
| | |

**8** Copy and solve each problem. Multiply to check your work.

| 5$\overline{)165}$ | 3$\overline{)237}$ |
|---|---|
| 4$\overline{)248}$ | 6$\overline{)192}$ |

**9** Solve one problem. Have a friend solve the other problem. Compare answers. Discuss why you think you got the same answers or different answers.

| 34 | 30 | 4 |
|---|---|---|
| x 5 | x 5 + | x 5 |

---

**Note to the teacher:** Program the student directions with the number of activities to be completed. Then copy the page and page 42 (back-to-back if desired) for each student.

# ═ Multiplication and Division of Larger Numbers ═

Name_____ Date_____

## Stocking Up

Multiply or divide.
Color the carrot with the matching product or quotient.

A. $2\overline{)114}$

B. $\begin{array}{r} 31 \\ \times\ 5 \\ \hline \end{array}$

C. $3\overline{)192}$

D. $\begin{array}{r} 26 \\ \times\ 4 \\ \hline \end{array}$

E. $7\overline{)280}$

F. $5\overline{)175}$

G. $\begin{array}{r} 19 \\ \times\ 4 \\ \hline \end{array}$

H. $6\overline{)468}$

Sale
Buy one, get
one FREE!

I. $8\overline{)736}$

J. $\begin{array}{r} 53 \\ \times\ 3 \\ \hline \end{array}$

35   81

40   92

57   104

64   155

76   159

K. $\begin{array}{r} 41 \\ \times\ 5 \\ \hline \end{array}$

L. $4\overline{)324}$

78   205

*Choose & Do Math Grids* • ©The Mailbox® Books • TEC61228 • Key p. 93

42   **Note to the teacher:** Use with page 41.

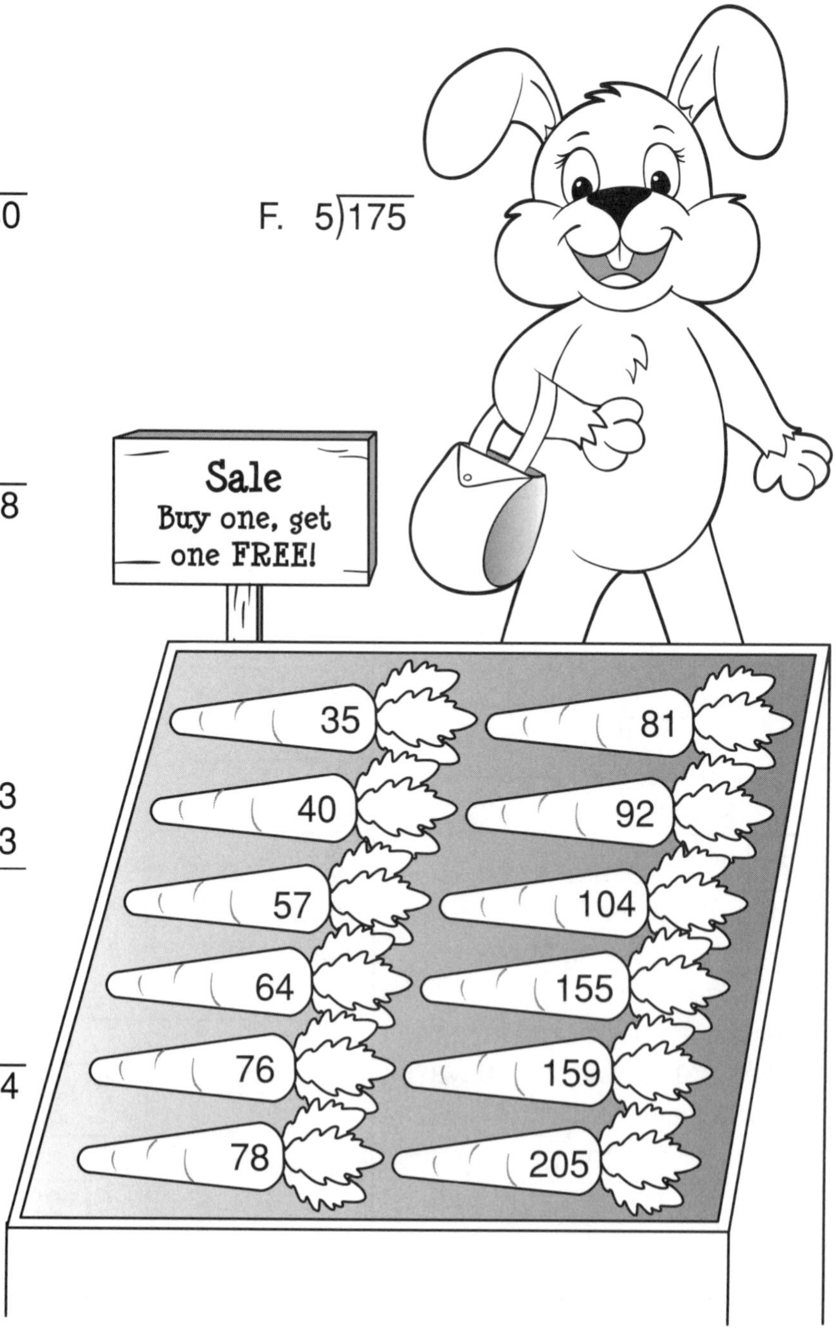

Name _____

Date _____

Choose ____ or more activities to do.
When you finish an activity, color its number.

| **1** Draw an analog clock to show each time. | **2** Show each time on an analog clock and a digital clock. | **3** Write the time to show 20 minutes later. |
|---|---|---|

**1** Draw an analog clock to show each time.

A. 4:20    B. 8:00
C. 11:15   D. 1:45
E. 7:05    F. 5:35
G. 2:50    H. 10:10

**2** Show each time on an analog clock and a digital clock.

A. half past three
B. nine o'clock
C. quarter past five
D. quarter to seven
E. noon

**3** Write the time to show 20 minutes later.

A. 1:30    B. 10:25
C. 4:50    D. 6:10
E. 8:35    F. 9:00
G. 2:05    H. 11:45
I. 3:15    J. 5:40

**4** Write each time. Draw a picture of something you might do at that time.

A. AM   B. PM
C. PM   D. AM

**5** Do the practice page "All That Jazz."

**6** Copy the pattern. Softly say the times aloud. Write the next five times. Draw an analog clock for each of the eight times.

1:45, 2:00, 2:15, ____,
____, ____, ____, ____

**7** Draw a clockface. Roll a die. Draw a minute hand pointing to the number rolled. Roll again. Draw an hour hand pointing to the number rolled. Write the time. Repeat five times.

**8** Tell what is wrong with this clock. Tell what time the clock should show.

3:60

**9** Make a schedule. List six things you do each day in order. Write the time for each one.

7:15 a.m.  Wake up for school.

**Note to the teacher:** Provide students access to a die to complete activity 7. Program the student directions with the number of activities to be completed. Then copy the page and page 44 (back-to-back if desired) for each student.

43

Name_____  Date_____

## All That Jazz

Write each time.
Find a pattern in each row.
Draw and write the last time in each pattern.

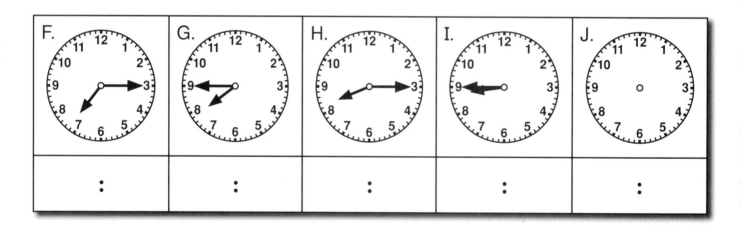

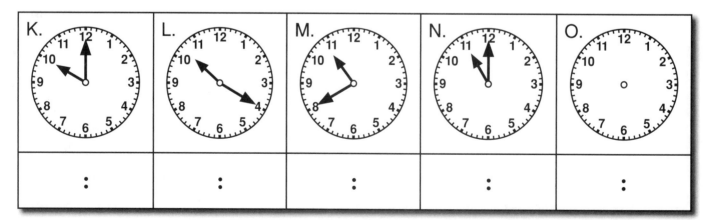

Name _____

Date _____

Choose ____ or more activities to do.
When you finish an activity, color its number.

| | | |
|---|---|---|
| **1** The minute hand is missing. What time could it be? Explain how you know.  | **2** Write the current time. Hop on one foot 30 times. Neatly write the alphabet two times. Write the current time. Draw clocks to show both times. | **3** Make a matching quiz. Draw eight clockfaces in a column on the left, each with a different time. Scramble the times in a column on the right. Make an answer key. |
| **4** Write every time that shows three numbers in order. Draw a clock to show each time. 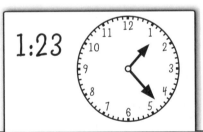 | **5** Do the practice page "Helping Hands."  | **6** There are only two times between 1:58 and 3:12 that have odd digits in all three places. Draw a clock to show each time. |
| **7** Write the time that is 1 hour, 10 minutes **before** each time.<br><br>A. 4:12　　E. 12:43<br>B. 6:56　　F. 10:31<br>C. 9:39　　G. 1:27<br>D. 8:16　　H. 3:44 | **8** Work with a partner to make a chart. Show the times you each wake up, do homework, eat dinner, and go to bed. Circle the earliest time for each task. | **9** Write all the times that have three digits that are the same. Draw a clock to show each time.  |

*Choose & Do Math Grids* • ©The Mailbox® Books • TEC61228 • Key p. 93

**Note to the teacher:** Program the student directions with the number of activities to be completed. Then copy the page and page 46 (back-to-back if desired) for each student.

45

Name _____

Date _____

# Time to One Minute

## Helping Hands

Draw the hour and minute hand on each clock.

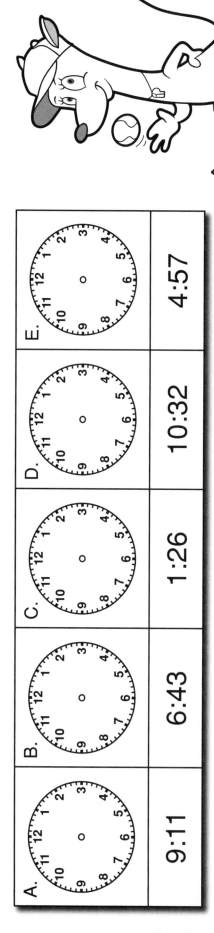

| A. | B. | C. | D. | E. |
|---|---|---|---|---|
| 9:11 | 6:43 | 1:26 | 10:32 | 4:57 |

| F. | G. | H. | I. | J. |
|---|---|---|---|---|
| 2:38 | 7:51 | 12:14 | 3:49 | 8:24 |

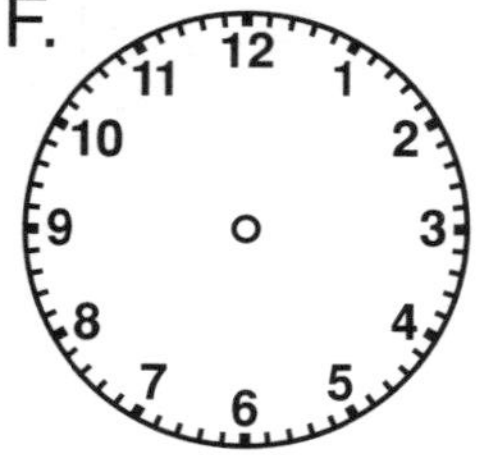

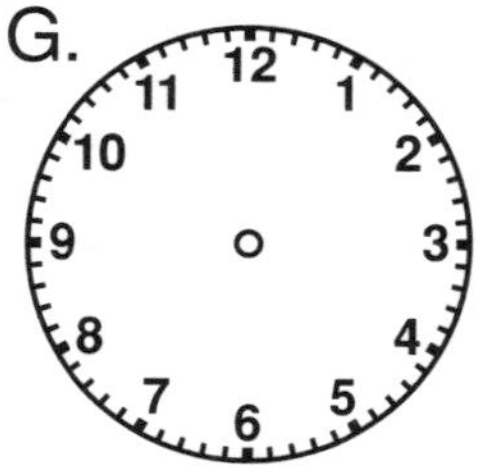

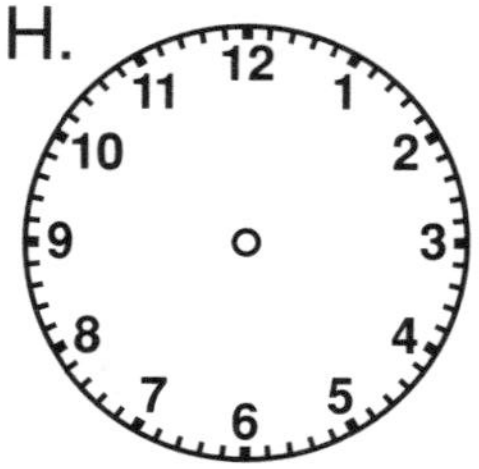

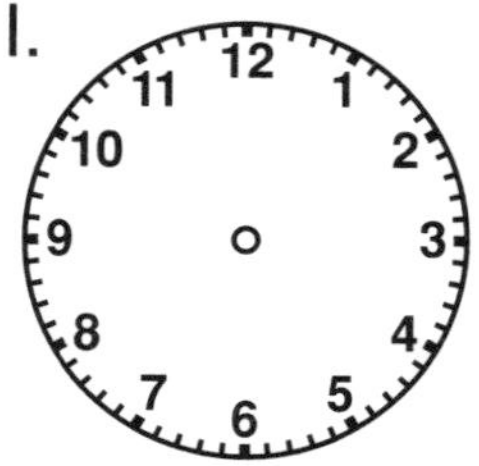

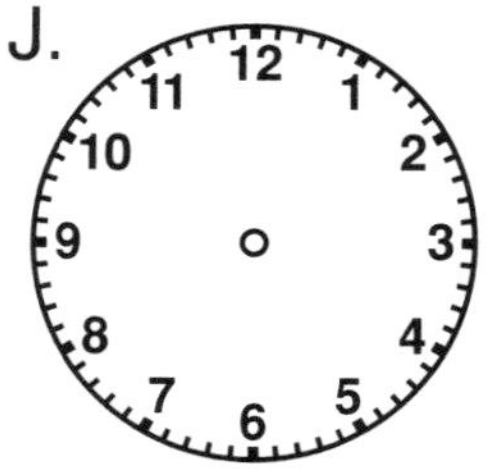

*Choose & Do Math Grids* • ©The Mailbox® Books • TEC61228 • Key p. 93

**Note to the teacher:** Use with page 45.

# Money to $1.00

Name _____

Date _____

Choose ____ or more activities to do.
When you finish an activity, color its number.

| **1** | Write the fewest number of coins needed to make each amount. |
|---|---|

A. 43¢　　　E. 26¢
B. 78¢　　　F. 56¢
C. 90¢　　　G. 14¢
D. 22¢　　　H. 65¢

| **2** | Write the name of each coin. How many of each coin do you need to make $1.00? |
|---|---|

A. 　　　B.
C. 　　　D.

| **3** | List five different ways to make 55¢. |
|---|---|

| **4** | Copy and complete the chart. |
|---|---|

| Price | Paid | Change |
|---|---|---|
| 29¢ | 50¢ | |
| 77¢ | $1.00 | |
| 56¢ | 75¢ | |
| 18¢ | 50¢ | |
| 35¢ | $1.00 | |

| **5** | Do the practice page "Planning a Salad." |
|---|---|

| **6** | Copy the problems. Then fill in the blanks. |
|---|---|

___ nickels = 3 dimes
___ quarters = 50 pennies
___ dimes = 12 nickels
___ nickels = 3 quarters
___ nickels = 8 dimes
___ pennies = 15 nickels

| **7** | There are eight coins in this bank. Work with a friend to figure out what they could be. |
|---|---|

72¢

| **8** | Copy. Find each total. Circle the greatest amount. |
|---|---|

A. 2 quarters and 1 dime
B. 9 nickels and 1 quarter
C. 1 half-dollar and 9 pennies
D. 6 dimes and 4 nickels
E. 30 pennies and 3 nickels

| **9** | Using only quarters, dimes, and nickels, how many different ways can you make 45¢? List each way. |
|---|---|

**Note to the teacher:** If desired, provide students with manipulative coins. Program the student directions with the number of activities to be completed. Then copy the page and page 48 (back-to-back if desired) for each student.

# Money to $1.00

Name_____   Date_____

## Planning a Salad

Show each amount.
Cross out the extra coins in each row.

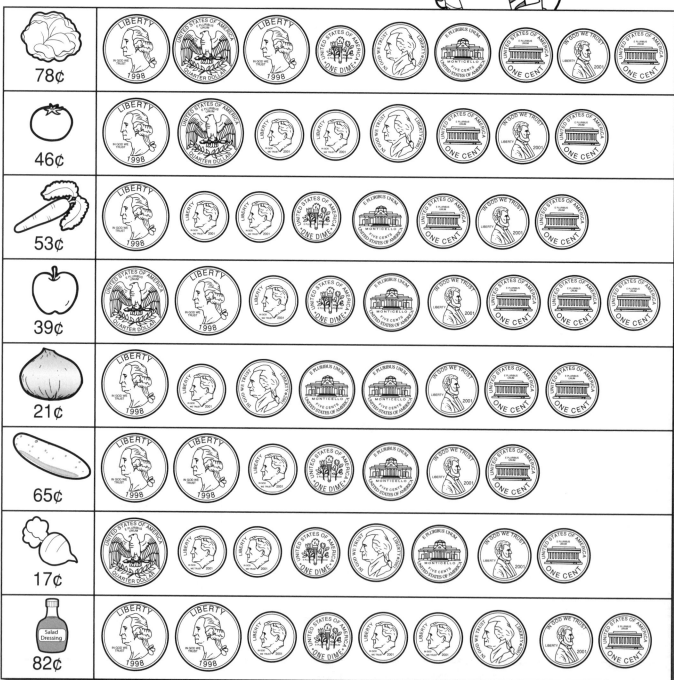

# Money to $5.00

Name _____

Date _____

Choose ____ or more activities to do.
When you finish an activity, color its number.

---

**1** Copy and complete the chart.

|         | 2    | 3   | 5    | 6 |
|---------|------|-----|------|---|
| penny   |      | 3¢  |      |   |
| nickel  |      |     | 25¢  |   |
| dime    | 20¢  |     |      |   |
| quarter |      |     |      |   |

**2** Using only dollar bills and quarters, how many ways can you make $4.50? List the ways.

**3** You want to spend $5.00. Which three items can you buy together and receive no change?

 $1.37  $1.92

 $2.14   $1.58

$1.71

**4** List two different ways to make each amount.

A. $4.61
B. $1.20
C. $3.55
D. $5.00
E. $2.32

**5** Do the practice page "Sandy's Snack Stand."

**6** Label a paper as shown. Cut the paper to make cards. Choose four cards and write the total. Repeat ten times.

| $1.00 | $1.00 | $1.00 | $1.00 |
|-------|-------|-------|-------|
| 50¢   | 50¢   | 25¢   | 25¢   |
| 10¢   | 10¢   | 5¢    | 5¢    |

**7** Write twelve equations. Use only coins. Each total must be greater than $1.00.

15 quarters = $3.75
22 nickels = $1.10

**8** If you used $5.00 to pay each amount shown, how much change would you receive?

A. $1.75
B. $2.30
C. $3.98
D. $4.24
E. 86¢

**9** Make a menu showing foods and their prices. Then write three word problems that can be solved using your menu.

---

*Choose & Do Math Grids* • ©The Mailbox® Books • TEC61228 • Key p. 93

**Note to the teacher:** Program the student directions with the number of activities to be completed. Then copy the page and page 50 (back-to-back if desired) for each student.

49

Name ______________________ Date ______________________

## Sandy's Snack Stand

Write the amount.
Write the matching snack.

A.

$ ______________

______________

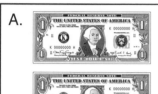

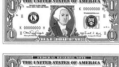

B.

$ ______________

______________

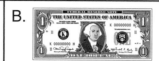

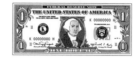

C.

$ ______________

______________

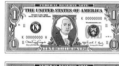

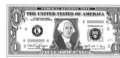

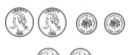

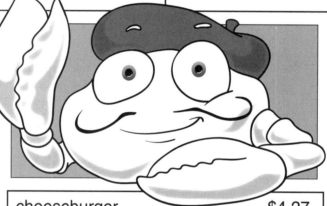

cheeseburger.............................$4.27
hot dog.......................................$4.17
nachos.......................................$3.63
pretzel........................................$2.80
popcorn......................................$2.37
cotton candy ..............................$3.06

D.

$ ______________

______________

E.

$ ______________

______________

F.

$ ______________

______________



 **Note to the teacher:** Use with page 49.

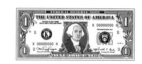

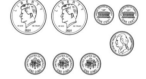

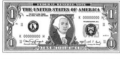

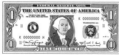

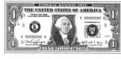

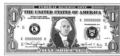

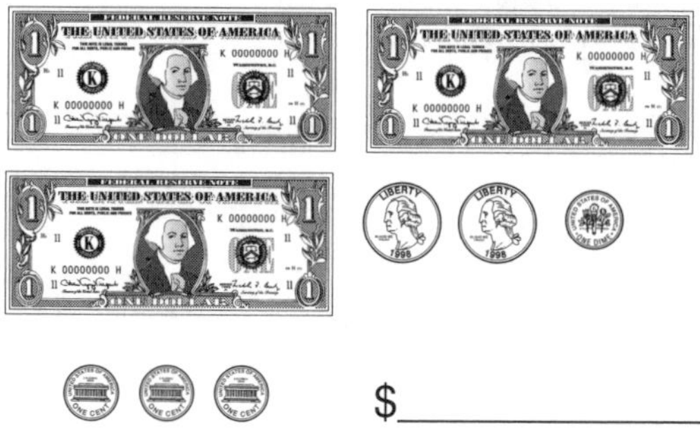

# Linear Measurement

Name _____

Date _____

Choose ____ or more activities to do.
When you finish an activity, color its number.
Measure to the nearest _____.

---

**1** Use a straight edge to draw eight lines of different lengths. Estimate the length of each line. Then measure and record the actual length.

**2** Search the room for objects that match each length. Complete the chart.

| Length | Object | Actual Measurement |
|---|---|---|
| 1_____ | | |
| 12_____ | | |
| 3_____ | | |
| 6_____ | | |
| 8_____ | | |

**3** How do you measure something that is longer than a ruler? Write the steps. To check your work, read the steps to a classmate. Have your pal use the steps to measure.

---

**4** What is the best unit to measure the length of each animal? Write _____ or _____ .

A. goldfish   E. dinosaur
B. giraffe    F. whale
C. alligator  G. worm
D. hamster    H. python

**5** Do the practice page "Gone Fishing."

**6** List six items inside your desk. Write the length of each to the nearest _____ .

---

**7** Copy and complete the chart. Add three objects.

| Object | Estimate | Actual Length |
|---|---|---|
| pencil | | |
| shoe | | |
| thumb | | |
| | | |
| | | |
| | | |

**8** Trace your hand and then number each fingertip on your drawing. Use _____ to find the distance from

A. 1 to 5
B. 3 to 4
C. 1 to 4
D. 2 to 5
E. 3 to 5

**9** Copy the chart. List ten items in each column.

| Shorter Than 10 | Longer Than 10 |
|---|---|
| _____ | _____ |

---

*Choose & Do Math Grids* • ©The Mailbox® Books • TEC61228

# Linear Measurement

Name_____    Date_____

## Gone Fishing

Measure each line to the nearest _____.

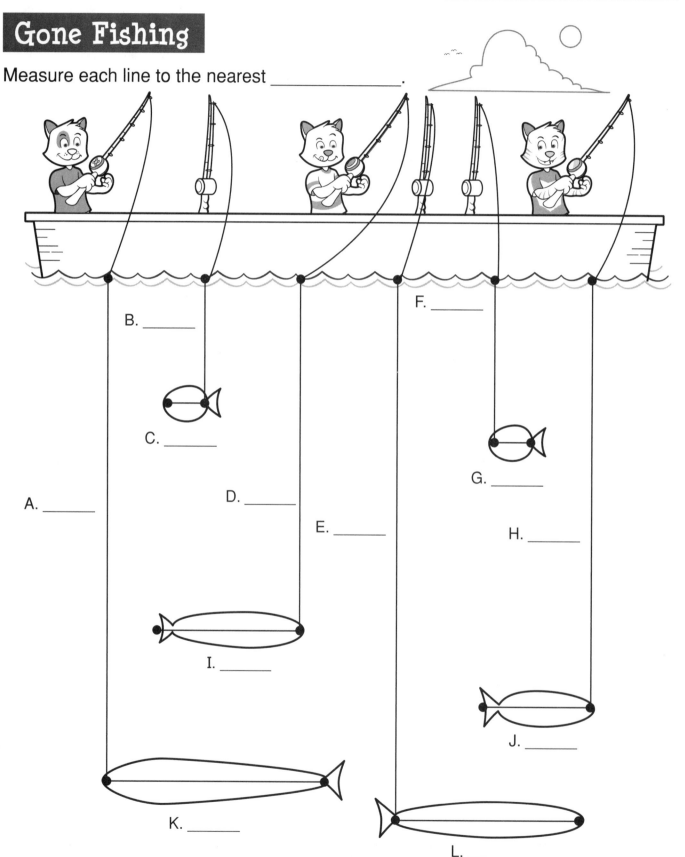

# Linear Measurement

Name _____

Date _____

Choose ____ or more activities to do.
When you finish an activity, color its number.
Measure to the nearest _____.

---

**1** Draw a house. Find the perimeter of the roof, door, window, chimney, and house.

**2** Write the alphabet in a long, straight line. Draw a • above each letter. Find the distance between

| | |
|---|---|
| **A and P** | **D and M** |
| **H and Y** | **B and L** |
| **O and Z** | **J and Q** |

•    •    •    •    •    •
Ȧ   Ḃ   Ċ   Ḋ   Ė   Ḟ

**3** Find and record the perimeter of each item.

A. **this square**
B. **this grid**
C. **this page**

**4** Record the length of your pencil. Find three items shorter than your pencil. Then find three items longer than your pencil. Measure and write the length of each item.

**5** Do the practice page "Follow the Map!"

**6** Draw six flowers of different heights. Estimate the length of each stem. Then measure and write the actual length.

**7** Pretend that both ends are broken off your ruler. Write to tell how you could still use it to find the length of this fish.

**8** Draw a large stick figure on your paper. Write the length of each straight line.

**9** Write clues to describe five objects. For each clue, include the object's length, height, or width. Ask a friend to guess your objects.

---

*Choose & Do Math Grids* • ©The Mailbox® Books • TEC61228 • Key p. 94

**Note to the teacher:** Program the top of the page with "inch" or "centimeter." Then program the student directions with the number of activities to be completed. Copy the page and page 54 (back-to-back if desired) for each student.

Name _____

Date _____

# Linear Measurement

## Follow the Map!

Measure each distance to the nearest half _____

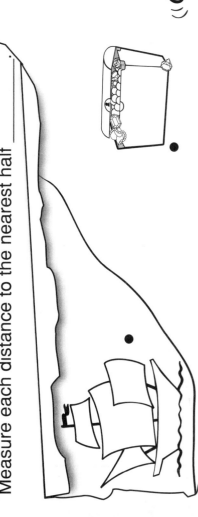

A. from ship to tree _____

B. from ship to X _____

C. from rock to tree _____

D. from tree to X _____

E. from X to chest _____

F. from ship to rock _____

G. from X to rock _____

H. from chest to rock _____

**Note to the teacher:** Program the directions with "inch" or "centimeter." Use with page 53.

# Capacity

Name _____

Date _____

Choose ___ or more activities to do.
When you finish an activity, color its number.

| **1** Draw each container. Tell which unit or units are best for measuring the liquid in each. | **2** Copy and complete the list. | **3** Make a capacity quiz. Use true-or-false questions. Make an answer key for the quiz. Then give the quiz to a friend. |
|---|---|---|
| pool     teacup<br>sink     bucket<br>fishbowl     pitcher<br>bathtub     vase | 2 quarts = ___ cups<br>3 pints = ___ cups<br>8 quarts = ___ gallons<br>8 pints = ___ quarts<br>1 gallon = ___ pints<br>4 cups = ___ quart | True or false?<br>2 pints = 1 quart   _true_ |

**1** Draw each container. Tell which unit or units are best for measuring the liquid in each.

pool     teacup
sink     bucket
fishbowl     pitcher
bathtub     vase

**4** Show four different ways to make one gallon.

**5** Do the practice page "Daisy's Dairy."

Milk

**6** Write ten inequalities. Use two different measurements in each. Use < or > in each one.

3 quarts < 1 gallon

**7** Write three riddles. Use clues to describe a pint, a quart, and a gallon.

I am a small unit.
There are 16 of me in a gallon.
What am I? _____

**8** Copy the chart. Write a different type of container in each space.

| Holds Less | Unit | Holds More |
|---|---|---|
|  | cup |  |
|  | pint |  |
|  | quart |  |
|  | gallon |  |

**9** Add one unit to each group to make one gallon.

A. two quarts, two pints
B. fourteen cups
C. six pints
D. seven pints, one cup
E. three quarts, one pint

**Note to the teacher:** Program the student directions with the number of activities to be completed. Then copy the page and page 56 (back-to-back if desired) for each student.

# Capacity

Name_____     Date_____

## Daisy's Dairy

Complete each chart.

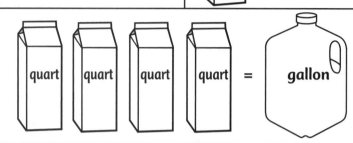

| A. | pints | 1 | 2 | 3 | 4 | 5 | 6 |
|----|-------|---|---|---|---|---|---|
|    | cups  |   |   | 6 |   |   | 12 |

| B. | gallons | 1 | 2 | 3 | 4 | 5 | 6 |
|----|---------|---|---|---|----|----|---|
|    | quarts  |   |   |   | 16 | 20 |   |

| C. | quarts | 1 | 2 | 3 | 4 | 5 | 6 |
|----|--------|---|---|---|---|---|---|
|    | pints  |   | 4 |   | 8 |   |   |

| D. | gallons | 1 | 2 | 3 | 4 | 5 | 6 |
|----|---------|---|----|---|---|----|---|
|    | pints   |   | 16 |   |   | 40 |   |

| E. | quarts | 1 | 2 | 3 | 4 | 5 | 6 |
|----|--------|---|---|----|---|---|---|
|    | cups   | 4 |   | 12 |   |   |   |

| F. | gallons | 1 | 2 | 3 | 4 | 5 | 6 |
|----|---------|----|---|---|---|---|----|
|    | cups    | 16 |   |   |   |   | 96 |

# Temperature and Weight

Name _____

Date _____

**Monday**
74°F
and
sunny

Choose ___ or more activities to do.
When you finish an activity, color its number.

| 1 | Draw and label a scene from each season. Tell what the temperature in each scene might be. |
|---|---|

| Winter | Spring |
|--------|--------|
| Summer | Fall |

| 2 | Copy the chart. List ten items in each column. |
|---|---|

| Less Than One Pound | More Than One Pound |
|---------------------|---------------------|
|                     |                     |

| 3 | Copy the chart. Name one outdoor activity you might do in each temperature. |
|---|---|

| 20°F | 60°F |
|------|------|
| 50°F | 80°F |
| 95°F | 32°F |

| 4 | Make a set of eight cards. On the front of each one, draw an item. On the back of the card, write whether the item's weight should be measured in ounces or pounds. Use your cards and a friend's cards to play a game. |
|---|---|

| 5 | Do the practice page "What's the Weather?" |
|---|---|

**Today's Weather**

68°F
and
sunny

| 6 | Draw six thermometers. Use a red crayon to show each temperature. |
|---|---|

| 60 |
|----|
| 50 |
| 40 |
| 30 |
| 20 |
| 10 |
| 0 |

10°F
45°F
30°F
20°F
25°F
5°F

| 7 | Copy the items. Tell whether to measure each one's weight in ounces or pounds. |
|---|---|

A. cat
B. cookie
C. car
D. pencil
E. bowling ball
F. television
G. dictionary
H. baseball

| 8 | Copy each sentence five times. Complete each sentence in a different way. |
|---|---|

A(n) _____ is heavier than a(n) _____.

A(n) _____ is lighter than a(n) _____.

| 9 | Write five questions that can be answered by studying the thermometers. |
|---|---|

| Day 1 | Day 2 | Day 3 |
|-------|-------|-------|
| 30 20 10 0 °F | 30 20 10 0 °F | 30 20 10 0 °F |

*Choose & Do Math Grids* • ©The Mailbox® Books • TEC61228 • Key p. 94

**Note to the teacher:** Program the student directions with the number of activities to be completed. Then copy the page and page 58 (back-to-back if desired) for each student.

57

# Temperature

Name_____  Date_____

## What's the Weather?

Write the temperature below each thermometer.
Then write the matching day of the week. Use the chart to help you.

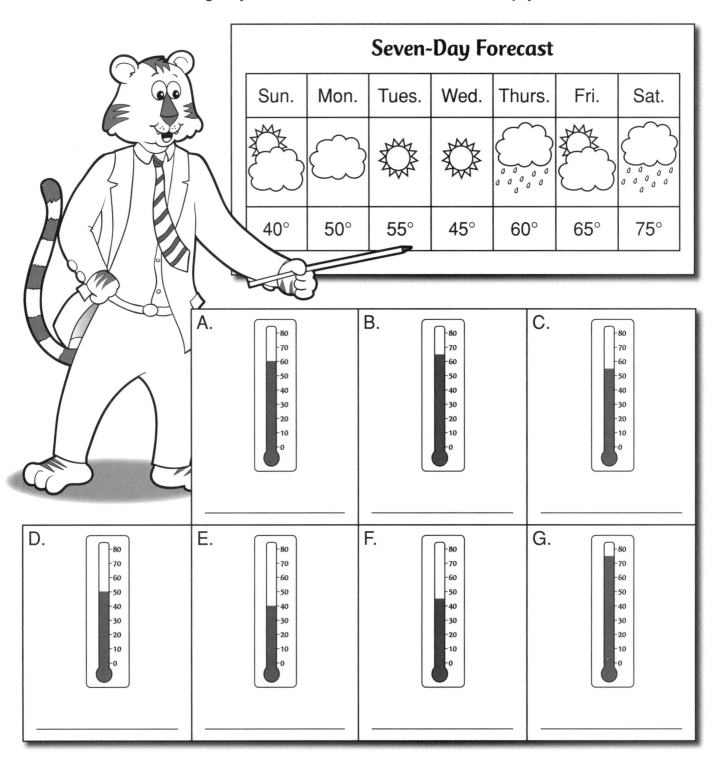

### Seven-Day Forecast

| Sun. | Mon. | Tues. | Wed. | Thurs. | Fri. | Sat. |
|------|------|-------|------|--------|------|------|
| 40° | 50° | 55° | 45° | 60° | 65° | 75° |

A.

B.

C.

D.

E.

F.

G.

# Number Patterns

Name _____

Date _____

Choose ____ or more activities to do.
When you finish an activity, color its number.

---

**1** Copy each pattern. Then write the next five numbers.

A. 3, 6, 9, 12...
B. 20, 25, 30, 35...
C. 90, 80, 70, 60...
D. 1, 4, 9, 16...
E. 31, 29, 27, 25...

---

**2** If the pattern continues, what will the weather be on the 17th? How do you know?

| April | | | | | | |
|---|---|---|---|---|---|---|
| S | M | T | W | Th | F | S |
| | | | | | | 1 |
| 2 | 3 | 4 | 5 | 6 | 7 | 8 |

---

**3** Copy the numbers. Softly say each number as the first number in a skip-count series to 30. If you say the number 24 as you are counting, circle the number.

A. 2     D. 5
B. 3     E. 6
C. 4     G. 7

---

**4** Study the torn hundred chart. Describe any patterns you see.

| 1 | 2 | 3 | 4 | 5 | 6 | 7 |
|---|---|---|---|---|---|---|
| 11 | 12 | 13 | 14 | 15 | 16 | |
| 21 | 22 | 23 | 24 | 25 | | |
| 31 | 32 | 33 | 34 | | | |
| 41 | 42 | 43 | 44 | | | |

---

**5** Do the practice page "Toads and Toadstools."

---

**6** Write the rule for each pattern.

A. 2, 4, 6, 8...
B. 30, 27, 24, 21...
C. 6, 16, 26, 36...
D. 5; 55; 555; 5,555...
E. 80, 70, 60, 50...

---

**7** Copy and complete the chart.

| Cars | 1 | 2 | 3 | 4 | 5 | 6 |
|---|---|---|---|---|---|---|
| Wheels | | | | | | |

---

**8** List three ways that you use number patterns.

1. I use number patterns when I multiply.

---

**9** Plan a movement pattern. Arrange a time with your teacher to teach the pattern to your class.

Snap, snap, clap, clap.
Snap, snap, clap, clap.
Snap, snap, clap, clap.

---

**Note to the teacher:** Program the student directions with the number of activities to be completed. Then copy the page and page 60 (back-to-back if desired) for each student.

Name _____  Date _____

# Number Patterns

## Toads and Toadstools

Fill in the missing numbers in each pattern.
Color each number as it is used.
Then write the rule for each pattern.

A. 14, 17, _____, _____, 26, 29, _____, 35, 38

Rule: _____

B. _____, 14, 12, 10, _____, 6, _____, 2, 0

Rule: _____

C. 3, 5, 8, 3, 5, 8, _____, _____,

Rule: _____

D. 45, _____, 55, 60, 65, _____, _____, 80, 85

Rule: _____

E. 1, 2, 4, 8, 16, _____, _____, 256

Rule: _____

F. 51, _____, _____, 39, 35, 31, 27, _____, 19

Rule: _____

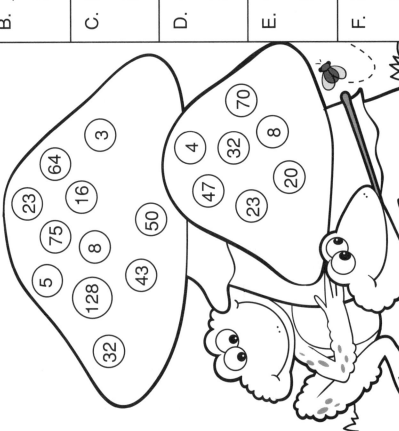

**Note to the teacher:** Use with page 59.

# Patterns

Name _____

Date _____

Choose ___ or more activities to do.
When you finish an activity, color its number.

---

**1** | Copy the chart. Study the pattern. Complete the chart.

| Figure | Number of Triangles | Number of Lines (\) |
|--------|---------------------|---------------------|
| △ | 1 | 3 |
| △▽ | 2 | 5 |
| ▽ | 3 | 7 |
|  | 4 |  |
|  | 5 |  |
|  | 6 |  |
|  | 7 |  |

**2** | Write to explain how this pattern changes. Draw the next figure in the pattern.

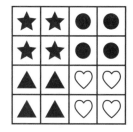

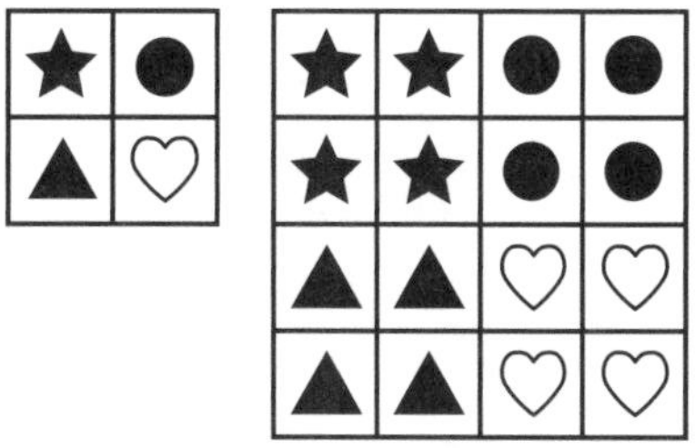

**3** | Draw a pattern on your paper. Write questions and answers about your pattern. Then show your pattern to a classmate. Ask your classmate the questions you have written.

What will the 15th shape be?

---

**4** | Design a pattern that uses only one of the shapes below. Write the rule for your pattern.

**5** | Do the practice page "Building Blocks."

**6** | Copy the necklace. Continue the pattern so it ends with four white beads.

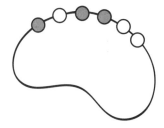

---

**7** | Make a book like the one shown. Draw a model of the pattern shown on each page.

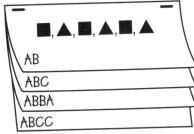
■,▲,■,▲,■,▲
AB
ABC
ABBA
ABCC

**8** | Copy each pattern. Cross out the mistake in each row. Draw the correct shape above each crossed-out shape.

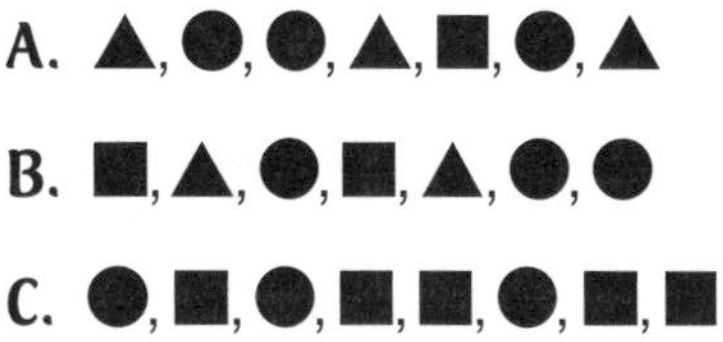

A. ▲●●▲■●▲

B. ■▲●■▲●●

C. ●■●■■●■■

**9** | Divide a paper into four sections. In each section, draw a pattern found in your classroom.

---

**Note to the teacher:** Program the student directions with the number of activities to be completed. Then copy the page and page 62 (back-to-back if desired) for each student.

# Patterns

Name_____  Date_____

## Building Blocks

Draw to complete each pattern.
Write the number of the matching
pattern rule.

**Pattern Rules**

| | | | |
|---|---|---|---|
| 1. | *AAB* | 5. | *AABC* |
| 2. | *ABA* | 6. | *ABBC* |
| 3. | *ABB* | 7. | *ABCC* |
| 4. | *ABC* | 8. | *ABBA* |

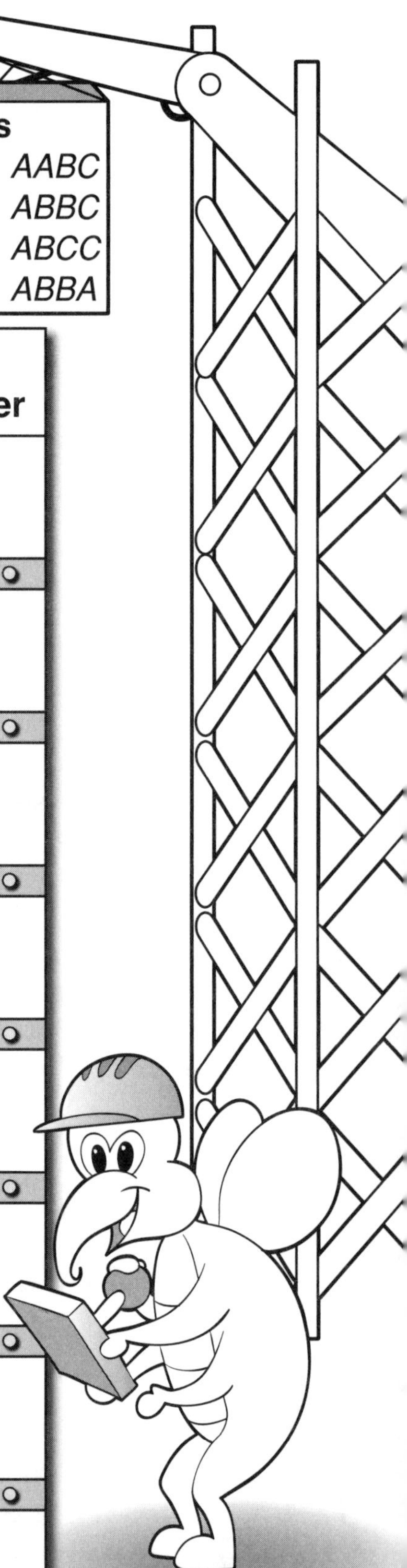

| Pattern | Rule Number |
|---|---|
| A.   __ ▱ △ △ __ △ __ ▱ | |
| B.   ◇ ⬡ __ ◇ ⬡ △ ◇ __ | |
| C.   ▱ ▱ ▱ __ __ ▱ ▱ ⬡ | |
| D. 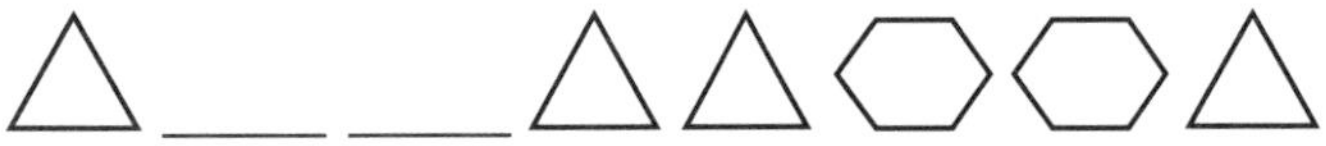  △ __ __ △ △ ⬡ ◇ △ | |
| E.   ▱ __ △ △ ▱ ◇ __ △ | |
| F.   __ ◻ ◻ ◇ ◻ ◻ ◇ __ | |
| G.   ⬡ ◇ __ ⬡ ◇ ⬡ ▱ __ | |
| H. 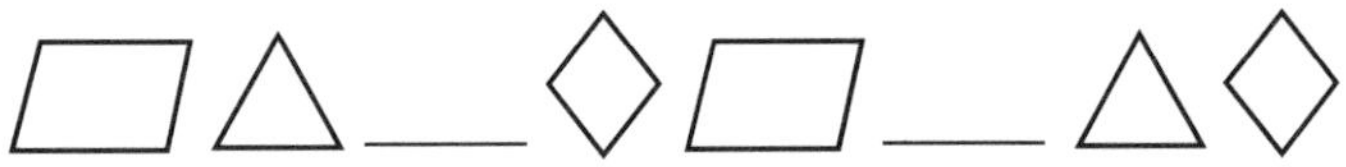  ▱ △ __ ◇ ▱ __ △ ◇ | |

# Properties

Name _____

Date _____

Choose ___ or more activities to do.
When you finish an activity, color its number.

| | | |
|---|---|---|
| **1** Draw a picture that shows that 7 + 6 = 6 + 7. How does this problem show the order property of addition? (Hint: this is also called the commutative property.) | **2** If you know that 9 + 7 = 16, how can you solve 7 + 9? Explain. | **3** Work with a partner to solve the problems. $$(7 + 3) + 4 =$$ $$7 + (3 + 4) =$$ What do the problems tell you about the associative property? Explain your answers to your partner. |
| **4** The associative property is also called the grouping property. Write to tell why this is a good name for it. | **5** Do the practice page "Freshly Picked." | **6** The identity property of addition is also called the zero property. How can it help you solve these problems? $$8 + 0 =$$ $$75 + 0 =$$ $$392 + 0 =$$ |
| **7** How does a number line help you explain the order property of multiplication? 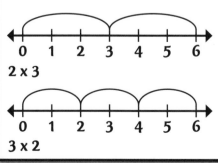 | **8** Show two different arrays for each problem. How do the arrays display the order property of multiplication? 4 x 2    3 x 5    6 x 1   4 x 2 | **9** Copy and solve the problems. 8 x 1    1 x 7 5 x 1    4 x 1 1 x 9    1 x 2 What do the answers tell you about the identity (one) property of multiplication? |

**Note to the teacher:** Program the student directions with the number of activities to be completed. Then copy the page and page 64 (back-to-back if desired) for each student.

63

# Properties

Name_____ Date_____

## Freshly Picked

Show the commutative property.
Write two problems on each bowl.
Use the numbers on the apples.

| A. | B. | C. |
|---|---|---|
| 3  7  21 | 48  8  6 | 5  10  2 |
| ___ X ___ = ___  ___ X ___ = ___ | ___ X ___ = ___  ___ X ___ = ___ | ___ X ___ = ___  ___ X ___ = ___ |

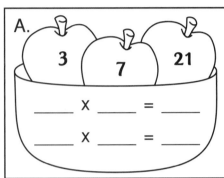 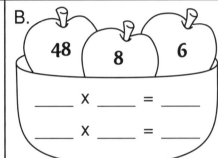 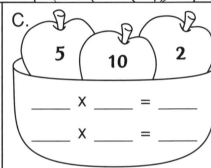

| D. | E. | F. |
|---|---|---|
| 9  7  63 | 3  12  4 | 42  6  7 |
| ___ X ___ = ___  ___ X ___ = ___ | ___ X ___ = ___  ___ X ___ = ___ | ___ X ___ = ___  ___ X ___ = ___ |

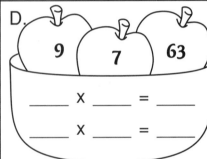 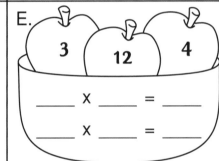 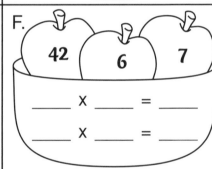

| G. | H. | I. |
|---|---|---|
| 6  18  3 | 9  5  45 | 4  7  28 |
| ___ X ___ = ___  ___ X ___ = ___ | ___ X ___ = ___  ___ X ___ = ___ | ___ X ___ = ___  ___ X ___ = ___ |

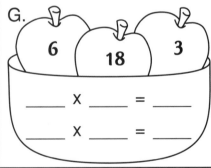 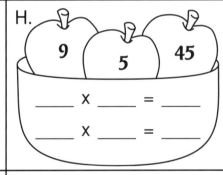 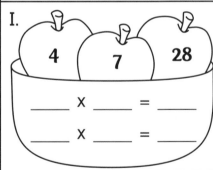

| J. | K. | L. |
|---|---|---|
| 2  8  16 | 1  9  9 | 15  5  3 |
| ___ X ___ = ___  ___ X ___ = ___ | ___ X ___ = ___  ___ X ___ = ___ | ___ X ___ = ___  ___ X ___ = ___ |

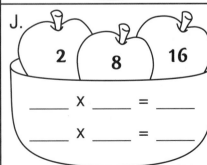 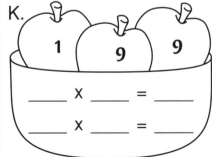

**Note to the teacher:** Use with page 63.

# Missing Variables

Name _____

Date _____

Choose ____ or more activities to do.
When you finish an activity, color its number.

| **1** Solve the number riddle. Then write one of your own.<br><br>**Subtract 4 from me and get 18. What am I?** | **2** Copy and solve each problem.<br><br>$7 + \square = 6 + 4$<br>$8 + 3 = \square + 6$<br>$5 + 5 = 2 + \square$<br>$9 + \square = 6 + 8$<br>$\square + 8 = 7 + 5$ | **3** Write + or − in each $\square$ to make the number sentence true.<br><br>$3\ \square\ 3\ \square\ 4\ \square\ 4\ \square\ 5\ \square\ 5 = 4$ |
| --- | --- | --- |
| **4** How can you find the missing numbers? Explain the steps to a classmate.<br><br>$9 + \square = 27$<br>$18 - \square = 11$ | **5** Do the practice page "Fiesta!"<br><br> | **6** Complete the square so that the sum of each column, row, and diagonal equals 15. Use each digit 1–9 only once.<br><br>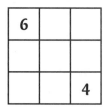 |
| **7** If the answer is 16, what could the question be? Write two possible word problems. | **8** Write the number 12. Then write six different number sentences that each equal 12.<br><br>$12$<br>$24 \div 2 = 12$ | **9** Copy and complete the chart.<br><br>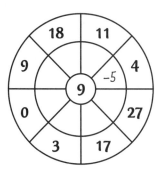 |

**Note to the teacher:** Program the student directions with the number of activities to be completed. Then copy the page and page 66 (back-to-back if desired) for each student.

# Missing Variables

Name_____     Date_____

## Fiesta!

Add or subtract.
Write the missing number in each .

A. $12 - $  $= 5$

B. $5 + $  $= 14$

C. $15 - $  $= 6$

D. $8 + $  $= 15$

E. $5 - $  $= 0$

F. $16 - 8 = $

G. $5 + $  $= 11$

H. $7 + $  $= 11$

I.  $- 6 = 10$

J. $12 - $  $= 8$

K.  $+ 6 = 14$

L.  $- 6 = 4$

M. $12 - 4 = $

N. $7 + $  $= 14$

O.  $+ 6 = 15$

Write $+$, $-$, or $=$ in each ☐ to make each pair of number sentences true.

P. $6 \; \square \; 4 \; \square \; 10$
   $10 \; \square \; 4 \; \square \; 6$

Q. $15 \; \square \; 7 \; \square \; 8$
   $8 \; \square \; 7 \; \square \; 15$

R. $13 \; \square \; 5 \; \square \; 8$
   $13 \; \square \; 8 \; \square \; 5$

S. $12 \; \square \; 8 \; \square \; 4$
   $8 \; \square \; 4 \; \square \; 12$

T. $5 \; \square \; 6 \; \square \; 11$
   $11 \; \square \; 6 \; \square \; 5$

# Fractions

Name _____

Date _____

Choose ___ or more activities to do.
When you finish an activity, color its number.

| | |
|---|---|

**1** | Copy the figure eight times. Color to show seven different fractions. Label each figure with its fraction.

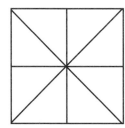

**2** | Draw a shaded figure to model each fraction.

| $\frac{1}{4}$ | $\frac{2}{3}$ | $\frac{3}{4}$ | $\frac{1}{2}$ | $\frac{1}{3}$ |
|---|---|---|---|---|

**3** | Write four or more sentences to tell about the pizza.

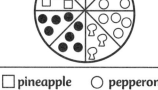

☐ pineapple   ○ pepperoni
● olive   ♀ mushroom

Mushrooms are on $\frac{1}{8}$ of the pizza.

**4** | Work with a friend and quietly decide whether a shape can be $\frac{1}{4}$ red, $\frac{2}{4}$ blue, and $\frac{3}{4}$ green. Write the reason for your answer.

**5** | Do the practice page "Born to Wrap."

**6** | Copy the figure ten times. Color each figure to show $\frac{2}{5}$ a different way.

**7** | Roll two dice. Write a fraction using the smaller number as the numerator and the larger number as the denominator. Then draw a model of the fraction. Repeat ten times.

**8** | Which figure shows $\frac{1}{3}$? Explain.

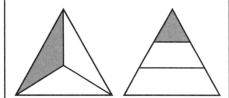

**9** | Fold a sheet of paper in half. Copy the chart on another paper. Complete the chart as you keep folding the paper.

| Folds | Sections | Number Sentence |
|---|---|---|
| 1 | 2 | $\frac{1}{2} + \frac{1}{2} = 1$ |
| 2 | | |
| 3 | | |
| 4 | | |

**Note to the teacher:** Program the student directions with the number of activities to be completed. Then copy the page and page 68 (back-to-back if desired) for each student.

# Fractions

Name_____ Date_____

## Born to Wrap

Color to match the fractions.

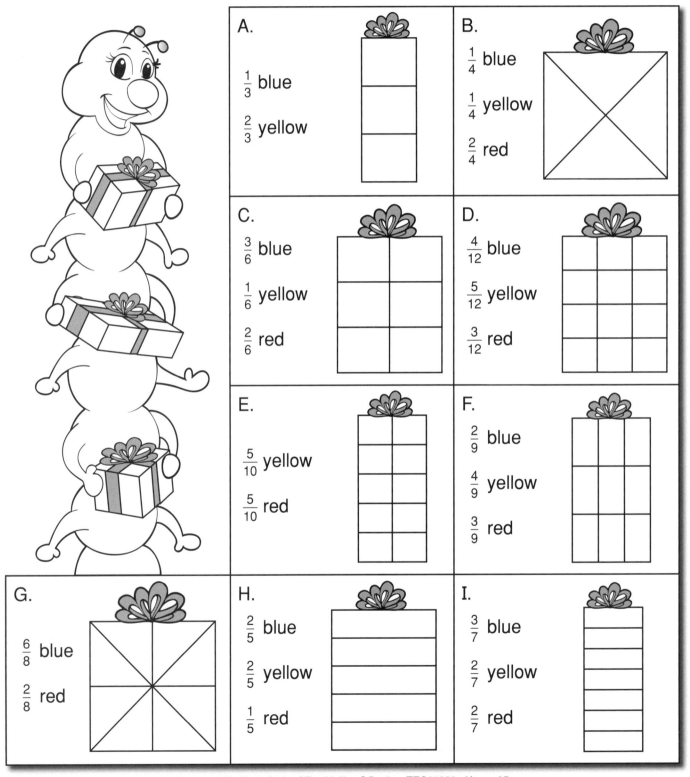

A.

$\frac{1}{3}$ blue

$\frac{2}{3}$ yellow

B.

$\frac{1}{4}$ blue

$\frac{1}{4}$ yellow

$\frac{2}{4}$ red

C.

$\frac{3}{6}$ blue

$\frac{1}{6}$ yellow

$\frac{2}{6}$ red

D.

$\frac{4}{12}$ blue

$\frac{5}{12}$ yellow

$\frac{3}{12}$ red

E.

$\frac{5}{10}$ yellow

$\frac{5}{10}$ red

F.

$\frac{2}{9}$ blue

$\frac{4}{9}$ yellow

$\frac{3}{9}$ red

G.

$\frac{6}{8}$ blue

$\frac{2}{8}$ red

H.

$\frac{2}{5}$ blue

$\frac{2}{5}$ yellow

$\frac{1}{5}$ red

I.

$\frac{3}{7}$ blue

$\frac{2}{7}$ yellow

$\frac{2}{7}$ red

# Fractions

Name _____

Date _____

Choose ___ or more activities to do.
When you finish an activity, color its number.

---

**1** Write a fraction for the shaded part of each rectangle. Write to tell how the fractions are alike and different.

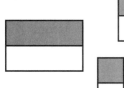

**2** Draw models to show each fraction. Cross out the fraction that does not belong. Write to tell why it does not fit.

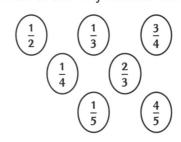

$\frac{1}{2}$ $\frac{1}{3}$ $\frac{3}{4}$
$\frac{1}{4}$ $\frac{2}{3}$
$\frac{1}{5}$ $\frac{4}{5}$

**3** Match a fraction on the top row with a fraction on the bottom row to make five pairs of equivalent fractions.

| $\frac{1}{2}$ | $\frac{2}{8}$ | $\frac{2}{6}$ | $\frac{1}{5}$ | $\frac{1}{6}$ |
|---|---|---|---|---|
| $\frac{2}{10}$ | $\frac{1}{3}$ | $\frac{1}{4}$ | $\frac{2}{12}$ | $\frac{2}{4}$ |

---

**4** Use the chart. Compare two fractions using <, >, or =. Repeat five times.

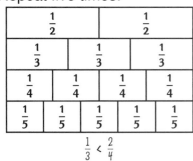

$\frac{1}{3} < \frac{2}{4}$

**5** Do the practice page "Quackers and Crackers."

**6** Name the shaded area. Write three fractions that are less. Write three fractions that are greater.

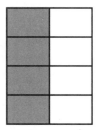

---

**7** Write two decimals for each fraction.

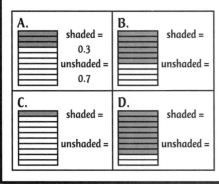

A. shaded = 0.3  unshaded = 0.7
B. shaded =  unshaded =
C. shaded =  unshaded =
D. shaded =  unshaded =

**8** Copy the number line. Make it as wide as your hand. Label the number line to show where each fraction belongs.

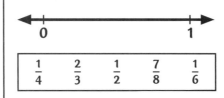

0      1

| $\frac{1}{4}$ | $\frac{2}{3}$ | $\frac{1}{2}$ | $\frac{7}{8}$ | $\frac{1}{6}$ |
|---|---|---|---|---|

**9** Write ten fractions that are equivalent to $\frac{5}{5}$. Explain to a friend what happens when the numerator and denominator are the same number.

---

**Note to the teacher:** Program the student directions with the number of activities to be completed. Then copy the page and page 70 (back-to-back if desired) for each student.

Name _____

Date _____

# Fractions

## Quackers and Crackers

Write a fraction for the shaded part of each cracker.

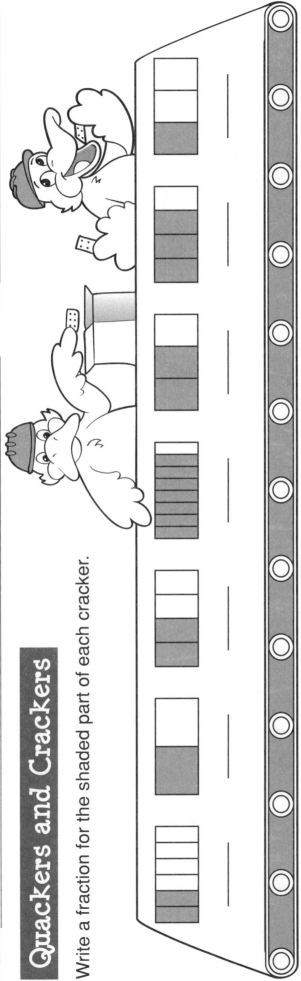

Write <, >, or =.

A. $\frac{1}{2}$ ◯ $\frac{1}{3}$

B. $\frac{7}{8}$ ◯ $\frac{1}{3}$

C. $\frac{1}{6}$ ◯ $\frac{7}{8}$

D. $\frac{2}{4}$ ◯ $\frac{3}{4}$

E. $\frac{7}{8}$ ◯ $\frac{3}{4}$

F. $\frac{1}{6}$ ◯ $\frac{1}{2}$

G. $\frac{1}{2}$ ◯ $\frac{2}{4}$

H. $\frac{3}{4}$ ◯ $\frac{2}{3}$

I. $\frac{2}{3}$ ◯ $\frac{4}{6}$

J. $\frac{1}{3}$ ◯ $\frac{3}{4}$

K. $\frac{3}{4}$ ◯ $\frac{1}{6}$

L. $\frac{2}{3}$ ◯ $\frac{1}{3}$

M. $\frac{1}{2}$ ◯ $\frac{7}{8}$

N. $\frac{1}{6}$ ◯ $\frac{2}{4}$

O. $\frac{2}{3}$ ◯ $\frac{1}{2}$

P. $\frac{1}{3}$ ◯ $\frac{1}{6}$

**Note to the teacher:** Use with page 69.

# Data and Graphs

Name _____

Date _____

Choose ___ or more activities to do.
When you finish an activity, color its number.

| **1** Use the clues to make a tally table. |
|---|

**Clues**
Wally sold snow cones on Friday. He sold 12 snow cones after lunch. He sold twice as many snow cones after dinner.

| **2** Is it better to use tally tables or pictographs to show data? Write three reasons to explain your choice. |
|---|

| **3** Write to tell what is missing from this pictograph. Tell why it is needed. |
|---|

| Flavor | Number |
|---|---|
| peach | ♉♉♉ |
| lime | ♉♉ |
| ♉ = 10 snow cones | |

| **4** Work with a partner. In turn, draw as many ♉ as you can in one minute. Use your data and your partner's data to make a pictograph. |
|---|

| **5** Do the practice page "Cool Treats." |
|---|

| **6** Survey your classmates. Find out whether they do or don't like snow cones. Show the results in a tally table. Then write two or more sentences about the data you collected. |
|---|

| **7** Write and answer three questions about the pictograph. |
|---|

### Snow Cones Eaten

| Student | Number |
|---|---|
| Wally | ♉♉♉♉♉ |
| Wanda | ♉♉♉ |
| ♉ = 5 snow cones | |

| **8** Who made more snow cones? Write to tell how you know. |
|---|

| | Winnie | | Will |
|---|---|---|---|
| Mon. | ‖‖‖ II | Mon. | ‖‖‖ ‖‖‖ |
| Tues. | IIII | Tues. | ‖‖‖ |
| Wed. | ‖‖‖ | Wed. | III |
| Thurs. | ‖‖‖ III | Thurs. | ‖‖‖ |

| **9** Pretend you have been asked to make a new page for your math book. Design a page that gives a meaning and an example for each term. Add color to make the page interesting. |
|---|

| data graph survey tally |
|---|

*Choose & Do Math Grids* • ©The Mailbox® Books • TEC61228 • Key p. 95

**Note to the teacher:** Program the student directions with the number of activities to be completed. Then copy the page and page 72 (back-to-back if desired) for each student.

71

# Data and Graphs

Name_____ Date_____

## Cool Treats

Follow the directions to complete
the pictograph below.
Use the tally chart.

1. Write a title for the graph.
2. Write the flavors.
3. Label the key so each 🍦 equals two snow cones sold.
4. Draw the snow cones.

**Saturday Snow Cone Sales**

| Flavor | Number Sold |
|--------|-------------|
| cherry | 卌 III |
| grape | 卌 卌 卌 I |
| lemon | 卌 |

_____

| Flavor | Number of Snow Cones Sold |
|--------|---------------------------|
|        |                           |
|        |                           |
|        |                           |
| 🍦 = |                           |

Write two sentences about the data. _____

_____

_____

# Data and Graphs

Name _____

Date _____

Choose ___ or more activities to do.
When you finish an activity, color its number.

| **1** | Survey your classmates. Find out how many of them think cats are good pets. Make a bar graph to show your results. |

| **2** | Use the data from the tally chart. Make a matching pictograph. |

| **Best-Selling Cat Toys** | |
|---|---|
| yarn balls | JHT JHT II |
| toy mice | JHT JHT |
| tunnels | JHT II |
| teasers | JHT JHT IIII |

| **3** | Write to tell how the graph would be different if it were a horizontal bar graph. Tell how it would stay the same. |

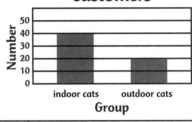

Customers

| **4** | Design a poster about pictographs. Tell why the title and key are needed to understand the graph. |

| **5** | Do the practice page "Finicky Eaters." |

| **6** | Copy the frequency table. Use the data to make a tally chart. |

| **Favorite Food Flavors** | |
|---|---|
| beef | 24 |
| tuna | 35 |
| chicken | 16 |
| salmon | 33 |

| **7** | Write five questions about the graph. Write the answers. |

March Toy Sales

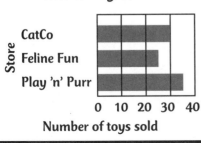

| **8** | Copy and complete the Venn diagram. |

Pictographs     Bar Graphs

Both

| **9** | Make a checklist that would help a classmate label all the parts of a graph. Write a meaning for each item on the checklist. |

☐ Title. It is at the top of the graph. It tells what the graph is about.

**Note to the teacher:** Program the student directions with the number of activities to be completed. Then copy the page and page 74 (back-to-back if desired) for each student.

73

# Data and Graphs

Name_____ Date_____

## Finicky Eaters

Use the data on the tally chart.
Make a bar graph.

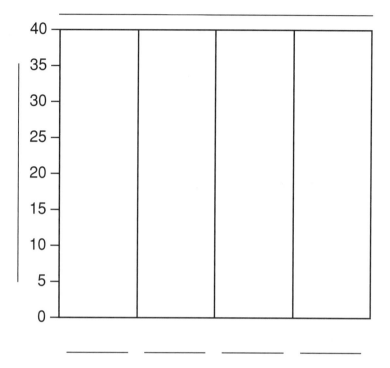

| Cats' Favorite Food Flavors | |
|---|---|
| beef | ⵀⵀ ⵀⵀ ⵀⵀ ⵀⵀ |
| tuna | ⵀⵀ ⵀⵀ ⵀⵀ ⵀⵀ ⵀⵀ ⵀⵀ |
| chicken | ⵀⵀ ⵀⵀ ⵀⵀ |
| salmon | ⵀⵀ ⵀⵀ ⵀⵀ ⵀⵀ ⵀⵀ |

Use the data above to answer the questions.

A.  How many cats chose tuna as their favorite flavor? _____

B.  How many cats chose chicken as their favorite flavor? _____

C.  Did more cats choose beef or salmon as their favorite flavor? _____

D.  How many more cats chose tuna than chicken? _____

E.  How many more cats chose tuna than beef? _____

F.  How many cats were surveyed in all? _____

# Probability

Name _____

Date _____

Choose ____ or more activities to do.
When you finish an activity, color its number.

| | | |
|---|---|---|
| **1** Write four or more sentences about the spinner. Use *more likely*, *less likely*, *certain*, and *impossible*. <br><br> (spinner: blue, brown, black) | **2** Make a list of five or more *certain* events in your classroom. Make a list of five or more *impossible* events. | **3** Pretend you put these chef hats in a bag. Draw the hat you are most likely to pick. Write to tell how you know. |
| **4** Look at the numbers. Copy and complete the sentences. <br><br> 2 2 4 4 6 8 8 8 8 8 <br><br> It is most likely I will pick ___. <br> It is least likely I will pick ___. <br> It is ___ I will pick an even number. | **5** Do the practice page "Mile-High Pizza Pie." | **6** Copy the chart. Flip a coin ten times. Draw a tally mark for each flip. Then write a sentence telling about your results. <br><br> | **heads** | | <br> | **tails** | | |
| **7** Draw the spinner. Write a different name in each section. Have a friend predict which name will be spun most. Then have your pal use a pencil and paper clip to spin the spinner ten times. Write about the results. | **8** Copy each sentence. Write *true* or *false* next to each one. <br><br> **It is possible to eat a pizza.** <br> **It is possible to hear a pizza.** <br> **It is impossible to see a mouse.** <br> **It is impossible to see a mouse fly.** | **9** Draw a bag with three cubes so that it is certain you will choose a blue cube. Draw a bag with four cubes so that it is most likely you will choose a red cube. Draw a bag with five cubes so that it is impossible to choose a green cube. |

**Note to the teacher:** Each student will need a coin to complete activity 6. Program the student directions with the number of activities to be completed. Then copy the page and page 76 (back-to-back if desired) for each student.

# Probability

Name _____

Date _____

## Mile-High Pizza Pie

Look at the spinner.
Answer each question.

1. Is this a fair spinner? _____ Why or why not? _____

_____

2. Which topping is most likely to be spun? _____

3. Which topping is least likely to be spun? _____

4. Is it *certain* or *impossible* to spin a pizza topping? _____

5. Is it *certain* or *impossible* to spin onions? _____

Use a paper clip and pencil to spin the spinner 20 times.
For each spin, color a square on the matching row.

| Topping | 1 | 2 | 3 | 4 | 5 | 6 | 7 | 8 | 9 | 10 | 11 | 12 | 13 | 14 | 15 | 16 | 17 | 18 | 19 | 20 |
|---------|---|---|---|---|---|---|---|---|---|----|----|----|----|----|----|----|----|----|----|----|
| sausage | | | | | | | | | | | | | | | | | | | | |
| peppers | | | | | | | | | | | | | | | | | | | | |
| mushrooms | | | | | | | | | | | | | | | | | | | | |
| pepperoni | | | | | | | | | | | | | | | | | | | | |

6. Write a sentence that tells about the results of your spins.

_____

*Choose & Do Math Grids* • ©The Mailbox® Books • TEC61228 • Key p. 95

**Note to the teacher:** Use with page 75.

# Plane Shapes

Name _____

Date _____

Choose ___ or more activities to do.
When you finish an activity, color its number.

| | | |
|---|---|---|
| **1** Design a poster. Draw and label six or more plane shapes. | **2** Tell how many squares and how many rectangles there are. | **3** Trace the hexagon three times. <br><br> **Draw lines to show six triangles.** <br> **Draw lines to show two trapezoids.** <br> **Draw lines to show two rhombuses and two triangles.** |
| **4** Draw a plane shape. Write a pattern of slides, flips, and turns. Repeat two more times. Make an answer key. Have a friend complete the pattern, and compare your pal's work to your key. <br><br> ■ → ___ → ___ → <br> flip    turn | **5** Do the practice page "Tuning In to Shapes." | **6** On a sheet of graph paper, draw a creature with at least one line of symmetry. Then draw a congruent creature. |
| **7** Copy the bowls. Write each capital letter of the alphabet in the matching bowl. <br><br> F — No Lines of Symmetry <br> A — One Line of Symmetry <br> H — Two or More Lines of Symmetry | **8** Cut a sheet of paper to make eight cards. Draw each shape shown on a different card and label it. <br><br> ● ▲ ■ ▮ ■ ◆ ⬡ ● <br><br> Sort the cards into two groups. Write the groups on another paper. Repeat. | **9** What do *symmetry* and *congruent* mean? How are they alike and different? Prepare your answer. Make plans to share your answer aloud with your teacher. |

*Choose & Do Math Grids* • ©The Mailbox® Books • TEC61228 • Key p. 95

**Note to the teacher:** Provide students access to graph paper to complete activity 6. Program the student directions with the number of activities to be completed. Then copy the page and page 78 (back-to-back if desired) for each student.

Name_____ Date_____

## Tuning In to Shapes

Complete the paragraphs below.
Use the shapes.

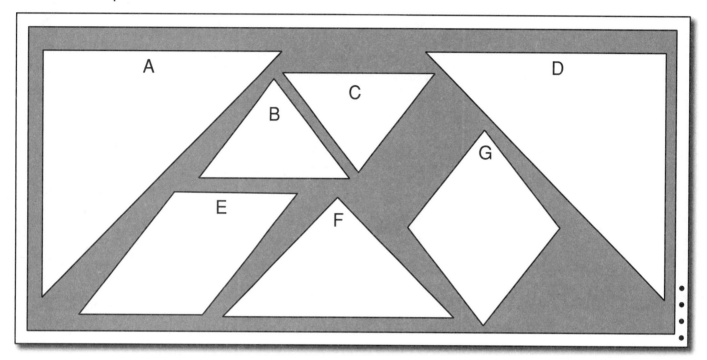

Shapes ___ and D are congruent shapes. This means they are the same size and shape. Shapes ___ and ___ are also congruent. If you move shapes B and C together to make one shape, that new shape would be congruent to shape ___. You could also put shapes B and C together in a different way to make them congruent to shape ___.

Shapes ___, ___, ___, ___, and ___ each have one line of symmetry. If you take a look at shape ___, you will see that it has two lines of symmetry. Shape ___ does not have any lines of symmetry.

# Plane Shapes and Solid Figures

Name _____

Date _____

face  vertex
edge

Choose ___ or more activities to do.
When you finish an activity, color its number.

| | | |
|---|---|---|
| **1** If you trace the bottom of a cylinder, you will draw a circle or oval. Can you trace the bottom of a sphere? Tell why or why not. | **2** Prepare a chant or rhyme that will help your classmates remember the difference between plane shapes and solid figures. Make plans with your teacher to share it aloud with the class. | **3** Copy the web. Write four solid figures. Then write a real-world example for each figure.<br><br>1.    2.<br>**Solid Figures**<br>3.    4. |
| **4** Make a Venn diagram. Compare and contrast plane shapes with solid figures.<br><br>Plane Shapes   Solid Figures<br>Both | **5** Do the practice page "Funny Faces." | **6** Choose two plane shapes and two solid figures. Write a riddle to describe each one. Read your riddles to a classmate. Challenge your pal to name each shape or figure. |
| **7** How many faces, vertices, and edges are there on one cube? If you put two cubes side by side to make one new figure, how many faces, vertices, and edges will you have? What is the name of the new figure? | **8** Choose five or more terms. Use them to write a math quiz. Include an answer key.<br><br>side   vertex   edge   face<br>sphere  circle  cube  square<br>quadrilateral    right angle<br>open figure   closed figure | **9** Copy each shape. If a shape has a right angle, use a crayon to trace one right angle. If a shape does not have a right angle, draw an X over the shape.<br><br>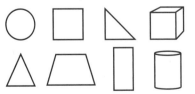 |

*Choose & Do Math Grids • ©The Mailbox® Books • TEC61228 • Key p. 95*

**Note to the teacher:** Program the student directions with the number of activities to be completed. Then copy the page and page 80 (back-to-back if desired) for each student.

# Plane Shapes and Solid Figures

Name_____  Date_____

## Funny Faces

Write the plane shape in the first column.
Write the name of a solid figure with that
    face in the second column.
Use the word bank.
Fill in the blanks to describe the solid figure.

| Plane Shape Face | Solid Figure | Solid Figure Description |
|---|---|---|
| 1. _____ | | __1__ face ___ vertex ___ edge |
| 2. _____ | | ___ faces ___ vertices ___ edges |
| 3. _____ | | ___ faces ___ vertices ___ edges |
| 4. _____ | | ___ faces ___ vertices ___ edges |
| 5. _____ | | __2__ faces ___ vertices ___ edges |
| **Word Bank** | | |
| circle    cone    cube    cylinder    oval    rectangle rectangular prism    square    triangle    triangular pyramid | | |

# Problem Solving

Name _____

Date _____

Choose ___ or more activities to do.
When you finish an activity, color its number.

| **1** Solve. Show your work. | **2** Draw a picture or a pattern to solve. | **3** Use the clues. Write each child's name in order from first to last. |
|---|---|---|
| **Crow took 28 stones out of the pitcher in the morning and 33 stones in the afternoon. There are still 14 stones in the pitcher. How many stones were in the pitcher to start?** | **Each female crow lays five eggs. How many eggs will there be if**<br><br>· there are two female crows?<br><br>· there are four female crows?<br><br>· there are eight female crows? | **Ty** saw the crow last. **Cal** saw the crow after **Hal**. **Pat** saw the crow after Cal. **Jim** saw the crow before Hal. |
| **4** Use the table to write and solve two story problems. | **5** Do the practice page "Clever Crow." | **6** What is missing from this problem? Write to tell why it is needed. |
| |  | **Crow is hungry. First he eats some nuts. Then he eats 11 more nuts. How many nuts does he eat in all?** |
| **7** Explain to a friend two different ways to solve the problem. Write the answer. | **8** Cut four paper cards. Write a different bird on each card. Use the cards to make a list and solve the problem. | **9** Copy the problem. Make a checklist that gives the steps to solve the problem using a hundred chart. |
| **Carrie watches birds for ten minutes each day all week long. How many minutes does she spend watching birds?** | | **A crow picks up 44 twigs to make its nest. It drops 17 twigs. How many twigs are left?** |

Table for activity 4:

| Crow's Name | Length (inches) |
|---|---|
| Cam | 22 |
| Carly | 15 |
| Caleb | 19 |
| Cole | 18 |

Cards for activity 8:

| crow | jay | finch | robin |
|---|---|---|---|

**If only two birds at a time sit on a fence, how many different pairs of birds could you see?**

**Note to the teacher:** Program the student directions with the number of activities to be completed. Then copy the page and page 82 (back-to-back if desired) for each student.

# Problem Solving

Name_____    Date_____

## Clever Crow

Read.
Solve.

A. Crow flew exactly 14 miles to get back to his nest. Trace his path.

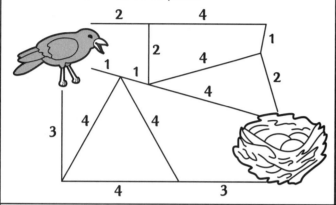

B. Crow flew 4 miles on Monday. Each day after that, he flew 3 more miles than the day before. How many miles did he fly on Friday?

| Day | Mon. | Tues. | Wed. | Thurs. | Fri. |
|-----|------|-------|------|--------|------|
| Miles | 4 | | | | |

C. How many stones did Crow remove from his pitcher from 12:30 to 1:30?

_____ stones

At what time did he remove the fewest stones?

_____

| Stones Removed | |
|-----|-----|
| Time | Number |
| 11:30 | 14 |
| 12:00 | 18 |
| 12:30 | 16 |
| 1:00 | 21 |
| 1:30 | 17 |

D. Crow has 78 nuts. He wants to have 100 nuts. After his friend Squirrel gives him 16, how many more nuts will he need?

E. Crow has 37 friends in the west and 43 friends in the east. How many friends does he have in all? _____ friends

How would your answer be different if Crow had 47 friends in the west and 33 friends in the east? Explain.

# Problem Solving

Name _____

Date _____

Choose ___ or more activities to do.
When you finish an activity, color its number.

| **1** Copy and complete the chart. Hint: when you add the numbers in each row or column, the sum should be 100. | **2** Solve the riddle. | **3** Rex learned 15 new tricks on Monday. Then he learned 23 tricks on Tuesday and 31 tricks on Wednesday. If this pattern continues, how many tricks will he learn on Thursday? How many will he learn on Friday? |
|---|---|---|

For activity 1:

| 50 |    | 16 |
|----|----|----|
|    | 42 | 28 |
| 20 | 24 |    |

For activity 2:

**I am an even number between 10 and 100. The sum of my digits is 9. What numbers could I be?**

| **4** Copy the pattern. Draw the next three shapes. Write to explain your choices. | **5** Do the practice page "Top Dog." | **6** Write and solve an addition story problem using these numbers. Then write and solve a subtraction problem using the same numbers. |
|---|---|---|

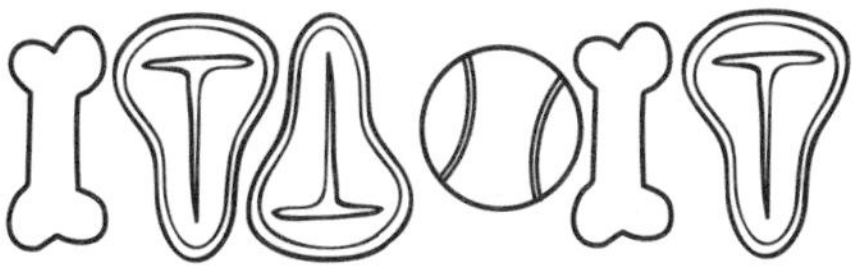

For activity 6:

| 750 | 250 |
|-----|-----|

| **7** Rex sorts his bones into piles of 100. If he has 972 bones, how many piles of 100 can he make? How many more bones will he need to make another pile of 100 bones? Write to tell how you know. | **8** Pretend today is Saturday, April 9. There will be a dog show in exactly two weeks. Write the day and date of the dog show. Then explain to a friend how you found the answer. | **9** Rex has 16 toys. He wants to equally share his toys with three playmates, but he also wants to keep some toys to play with. How many toys will each dog have? Draw a picture to show your answer. |
|---|---|---|

*Choose & Do Math Grids* • ©The Mailbox® Books • TEC61228 • Key p. 96

**Note to the teacher:** Program the student directions with the number of activities to be completed. Then copy the page and page 84 (back-to-back if desired) for each student.

83

Name _____

Date _____

# Problem Solving

## Top Dog

Read.
Solve.
Cross out the matching answer.

Numbers on trophy: 52, 61, 70, 534, 822

A. The dog show is 225 miles from Rex's house. He travels 80 miles on Monday and 75 miles on Tuesday. How many more miles does he need to travel to get to the dog show?

_____ miles

B. When Rex gets to the dog show, he learns that 355 dogs had planned to compete but only 294 dogs are there. How many dogs did not show up to compete?

_____ dogs

C. The dog show draws a big crowd. 483 tickets are sold in advance. 339 tickets are sold at the door. How many tickets are sold in all?

_____ tickets

D. Rex wins bones at the dog show. He wins 178 bones for winning his group. He wins 356 more bones for being the top dog in the entire show. How many bones does he win in all?

_____ bones

E. Rex won 67 shows when he was a puppy. So far, he has won 119 shows as an adult. How many more shows has Rex won as an adult than as a puppy?

_____ shows

**Note to the teacher:** Use with page 83.

# Problem Solving

Name _____

Date _____

Choose ___ or more activities to do.
When you finish an activity, color its number.

| | | |
|---|---|---|
| **1** Use the clues. Write the names and birthdays in order. | **2** Penny's favorite toy has at least one square face. Write two solid shapes the toy could be. Write two solid shapes the toy could not be. | **3** This is a drawing of Percy's pigpen. What is the perimeter of his pen? What is the area of his pen? Show your work. |

**1** Use the clues. Write the names and birthdays in order.

> *Penny was born five days after Porky. Porky was born on May 14. Percy was born 8 days before Porky. Prissy was born two weeks after Penny.*

**3** This is a drawing of Percy's pigpen. What is the perimeter of his pen? What is the area of his pen? Show your work.

13 ft.

8 ft.

**4** Porky has 65 cookies. He puts them into seven equal groups. How many cookies are in each group? How many cookies are left? Show two ways to solve the problem.

**5** Do the practice page "Rolling in Dough."

**6** Prissy likes to visit the bakery. Each time she goes, she walks nine feet. How many yards does she travel? How many inches?

> **12 inches = 1 foot**
> **3 feet = 1 yard**

**7** The pigs know they should always swim with a buddy. Work with a friend to make as many different pairs of pigs as possible. Write each pair.

| Porky | Prissy |
|---|---|
| Penny | Percy |

**8** Circle the important details. Cross out the unneeded details. Solve.

> *Percy has four feet. On each foot, he has four toes. Percy also has a tail. How many toes does Percy have in all?*

**9** There are 12 piglets. Penny watches six of them, Porky watches two of them, and Prissy watches the rest. Write a fraction to name the number of piglets each pig watches.

*Choose & Do Math Grids • ©The Mailbox® Books • TEC61228 • Key p. 96*

**Note to the teacher:** Program the student directions with the number of activities to be completed. Then copy the page and page 86 (back-to-back if desired) for each student.

85

# Problem Solving

Name ______________________________ Date ______________

## Rolling in Dough

Use the data from the table to solve each problem.
Show your work in the matching lettered box below.

A. How many brownies and coffee cakes were sold? _______

B. How many pies and sweet rolls were sold? _______

C. How many cookies, muffins, and tarts were sold? _______

D. What number would be on the table if half as many tarts had been sold? _______

E. How many more cookies than sweet rolls were sold? _______

F. How many more muffins than coffee cakes were sold? _______

G. What number would be on the table if twice as many pies had been sold? _______

H. How many pastries were sold in all? _______

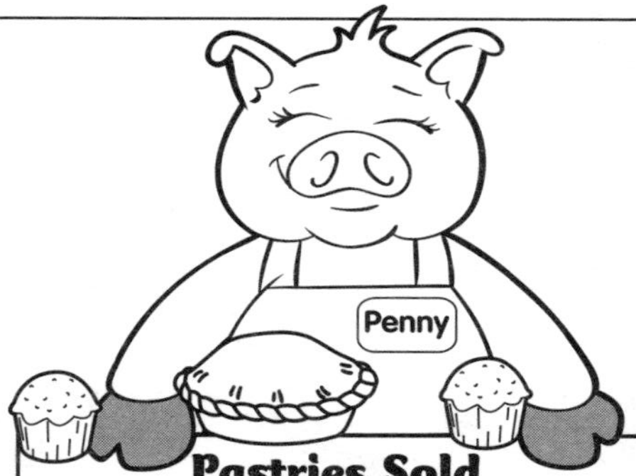

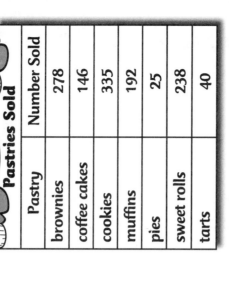

**Pastries Sold**

| Pastry | Number Sold |
|---|---|
| brownies | 278 |
| coffee cakes | 146 |
| cookies | 335 |
| muffins | 192 |
| pies | 25 |
| sweet rolls | 238 |
| tarts | 40 |

| A. | B. | C. | D. | E. | F. | G. | H. |
|---|---|---|---|---|---|---|---|
| | | | | | | | |



**Note to the teacher:** Use with page 85.

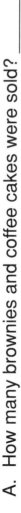

# Problem Solving

Name _____

Date _____

Choose ___ or more activities to do.
When you finish an activity, color its number.

| **1** Copy the puzzle. Use the rules to fill in each square. | **2** If a circle is folded in half two times, what will it look like? Draw pictures to show the circle at the beginning, after one fold, and after two folds. | **3** How many ways can 50¢ be made without using pennies? Make a chart to support your answer. |

**1**

Rules: → add 32
↓ subtract 28

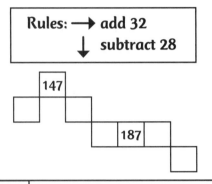

**3**

| Quarters | Dimes | Nickels |
|----------|-------|---------|
|          |       |         |
|          |       |         |
|          |       |         |
|          |       |         |
|          |       |         |
|          |       |         |
|          |       |         |
|          |       |         |
|          |       |         |

**4** Draw a Venn diagram to solve.

**Today the Snack Shack sold lunch to 24 customers. It sold 17 pizzas and 14 salads. 7 of the customers bought both pizza and salad. How many customers bought just pizza and how many bought just salad?**

**5** Do the practice page "Surf's Up!"

Sunscreen

**6** There are a total of 19 bicycles and tricycles at the beach. There are 45 wheels. How many bicycles are at the beach? How many tricycles are there? Show your work.

**7** Work with a partner. Write a different digit (1–8) in each circle. Add each line of three numbers. If the sum for each line is not 15, try again.

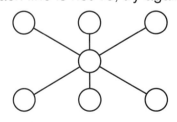

**8** One van holds a driver and six riders. If 28 riders want to visit the beach, how many vans are needed? Write to tell how you know.

**9** Draw a picture to solve.

**Dan has six coins. $\frac{1}{3}$ of the coins are dimes. The value of the dimes is $\frac{1}{4}$ the value of the coins. What are the coins?**

*Choose & Do Math Grids* • ©The Mailbox® Books • TEC61228 • Key p. 96

**Note to the teacher:** Program the student directions with the number of activities to be completed. Then copy the page and page 88 (back-to-back if desired) for each student.

87

# Problem Solving

Name_____ Date_____

## Surf's Up!

Solve each problem.
Show your work on another paper.

A. Dan Dolphin has surfed for 7 years. His brother, Dave, has surfed 8 years longer than Dan. How many years have the brothers surfed in all?

_____

B. Dan doesn't know what to wear. He has red sunglasses and blue sunglasses, a yellow shirt and a green shirt, and purple shorts and black shorts. How many different outfits can he make?

_____

C. Dan surfs every other day. Dave surfs every three days. If they surf together one day, how many days will it be until they surf together again?

_____

D. Three of Dan's wetsuits cost as much as one surfboard. If a wetsuit costs $94.61, how much does a surfboard cost?

_____

E. The number of beach visitors is between 200 and 300. The hundreds and tens digits are the same. The ones digit is double the sum of the hundreds and tens digits. How many beach visitors are there?

_____

F. Dan spent $\frac{1}{3}$ of the day surfing. Dave spent $\frac{1}{4}$ of the day surfing. Who spent more time surfing?

_____

G. There are 7 kayaks to rent. Dave and 20 of his friends want to go kayaking. If each kayak holds 4 kayakers, how many kayaks will they need? _____ Are there enough?

_____

H. There are 18 sandals in the sand. How many pairs of sandals are in the sand?

_____

*Choose & Do Math Grids* • ©The Mailbox® Books • TEC61228 • Key p. 96

**Note to the teacher:** Use with page 87.

Name _____

Date _____

Choose ___ or more activities to do.
When you finish an activity, color its number.

| 1 | 2 | 3 |
|---|---|---|
| 4 | 5 | 6 |
| 7 | 8 | 9 |

*Choose & Do Math Grids* • ©The Mailbox® Books • TEC61228

**Page 5**

4, 7–9. Answers may vary.

1. 456, 466, 476, 486, 496, 506, 516, 526, 536, 546, 556, 566, 576, 586, 596, 606, 616, 626, 636, 646, 656, 666, 676, 686, 696, 706, 716, 726

2.

| Hundreds | Tens | Ones | Number |
|---|---|---|---|
| four | three | two | 432 |
| seven | nine | one | 791 |
| six | five | two | 652 |
| eight | zero | three | 803 |
| two | three | seven | 237 |

3. 35, 37, 39, 41, 43, 45, 47, 49, 51, 53, 55, 57, 59, 61, 63, 65, 67, 69, 71, 73, 75, 77, 79

6. 13 = [model]   103 = [model]   130 = [model]
   If 103 and 130 did not have zeros, all three models would show 13.

**Page 6**

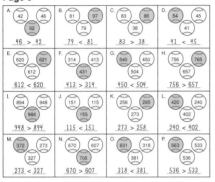

A. 46 > 42
B. 79 < 81
C. 83 > 38
D. 41 < 45
E. 612 < 620
F. 413 > 314
G. 450 < 504
H. 756 > 657
I. 948 > 894
J. 115 < 151
K. 273 > 258
L. 240 < 402
M. 273 < 327
N. 670 > 607
O. 318 < 381
P. 536 > 533

**Page 7**

1, 6, 7. Answers may vary.
2. Order may vary.
   even: 1,002; 3,156; 8,480; 6,374
   odd: 4,737; 2,641; 1,599; 9,945

3.

| Number | + 10 | + 100 | + 1,000 |
|---|---|---|---|
| 619 | 629 | 719 | 1,619 |
| 4,201 | 4,211 | 4,301 | 5,201 |
| 35 | 45 | 135 | 1,035 |
| 972 | 982 | 1,072 | 1,972 |
| 5,614 | 5,624 | 5,714 | 6,614 |

4. 4,2<u>8</u>5 = 80        7,<u>5</u>03 = 500
   <u>2</u>,109 = 2,000     3,6<u>1</u>8 = 10
   7,<u>6</u>39 = 600        1,72<u>4</u> = 4
   <u>8</u>,402 = 8,000     <u>5</u>,091 = 5,000

8. [number line] 0  250  985 1,240  2,531  3,045  4,923 5,000

9. 1,734; 1,834; 1,934; 2,034; 2,134; 2,234; 2,334; 2,434; 2,534; 2,634; 2,734; 2,834; 2,934; 3,034

**Page 8**

A. red       B. pink      C. orange   D. purple   E. blue      F. yellow
G. purple  H. yellow   I. red          J. brown    K. pink      L. green
M. blue    N. brown    O. blue        P. green    Q. yellow   R. orange
S. orange  T. green    U. purple    V. pink       W. red        X. brown

**Page 9**

7–9. Answers may vary.
1. Order may vary. 25,679; 25,697; 25,769; 25,796; 25,967; 25,976; 26,579; 26,597; 26,759; 26,795
2. 24,710 = 24,700   65,299 = 65,300
   83,208 = 83,200   14,854 = 14,900
   77,493 = 77,500   27,390 = 27,400
   20,681 = 20,700   62,584 = 62,600
3. 43,219 = 40,000 + 3,000 + 200 + 10 + 9
   86,745 = 80,000 + 6,000 + 700 + 40 + 5
   18,875 = 10,000 + 8,000 + 800 + 70 + 5
   37,021 = 30,000 + 7,000 + 20 + 1
   56,940 = 50,000 + 6,000 + 900 + 40
4. You could put 3, 4, 5, 6, 7, 8, or 9 in the □. All the other digits in both numbers are the same. Since the first number must be greater than the second number, the number in its hundreds place should be greater than the 2 in the second number's hundreds place.

6.

| Number Before | 😊 | Number After |
|---|---|---|
| 45,898 | 45,899 | 45,900 |
| 20,411 | 20,412 | 20,413 |
| 73,739 | 73,740 | 73,741 |
| 91,355 | 91,356 | 91,357 |
| 16,002 | 16,003 | 16,004 |

**Page 10**

A. 10,617      G. 62,930
B. 23,516      H. 74,183
C. 32,587      I. 75,024
D. 49,245      J. 88,436
E. 49,315      K. 90,237
F. 52,756      L. 96,485

**Page 11**

1. Answers may vary.
2. 5 or 13
   4 + 5 = 9    4 + 9 = 13
   5 + 4 = 9    9 + 4 = 13
   9 − 4 = 5    13 − 4 = 9
   9 − 5 = 4    13 − 9 = 4
3. 2 + 6 = 8, 2 + 3 = 5, 2 + 8 = 10, 2 + 5 = 7, 7 + 6 = 13, 7 + 3 = 10, 7 + 8 = 15, 7 + 5 = 12, 4 + 6 = 10, 4 + 3 = 7, 4 + 8 = 12, 4 + 5 = 9, 9 + 6 = 15, 9 + 3 = 12, 9 + 8 = 17, 9 + 5 = 14
4. 8 + 6 = 14, 15 − 7 = 8, 13 − 6 = 7, 9 + 7 = 16, 5 + 8 = 13
6. 14 − 8 = 6, 14 − 5 = 9, 8 − 5 = 3; 12 − 8 = 4, 12 − 3 = 9, 8 − 3 = 5; 15 − 6 = 9, 15 − 8 = 7, 8 − 6 = 2
7. 6 + 5 = 11; 5 + 5 + 1, or 6 + 6 − 1
   8 + 9 = 17; 8 + 8 + 1, or 9 + 9 − 1
   5 + 7 =12; 5 + 5 + 2, or 7 + 7 − 2
   7 + 8 = 15; 7 + 7 + 1, or 8 + 8 − 1
8. Related facts have the same addends, but in a different order, and make the same sum. Both facts have the same sum, but they do not have the same addends.
9. 11 − 4 = 7, 13 − 8 = 5, 14 − 5 = 9
   15 − 9 = 6, 16 − 9 = 7, 17 − 8 = 9

**Page 12**

Order may vary.

A. 6 + 7 = 13      B. 4 + 8 = 12      C. 10 − 3 = 7       D. 14 − 9 = 5
   7 + 6 = 13          12 − 4 = 8          10 − 7 = 3            9 + 5 = 14
   13 − 7 = 6          8 + 4 = 12          7 + 3 = 10            14 − 5 = 9
   13 − 6 = 7          12 − 8 = 4          3 + 7 = 10            5 + 9 = 14

**Page 13**

1, 6, 8, 9. Answers may vary.
2.
   63      19      26
 + 27    + 35    + 58
 ----    ----    ----
   90      54      84

3. Order of addends may vary.
   25      (29)     36
 + 57    (+ 29)   + 48
 ----    ----     ----
   82      (58)     84

4.
   28      28      17      45
 + 17    + 45    + 17    + 45
 ----    ----    ----    ----
   45      73      34      90

7.   75 shows regrouping.
   + 19

**Page 14**

A. 45      B. 72      C. 73      D. 33      E. 57
F. 63      G. 75      H. 62      I. 71       J. 54
K. 51      L. 72      M. 31      N. 93      O. 91

**Page 15**

1, 7. Answers may vary.
2. △ = 6, 7, 8, or 9   □ = 5, 6, 7, 8, or 9
3. A = 1, B = 2, C = 3, D = 4, E = 5, F = 6, G = 7, H = 8, I = 9, J = 10, K = 11, L = 12, M = 13, N = 14, O = 15, P = 16, Q = 17, R = 18, S = 19, T = 20, U = 21, V = 22, W = 23, X = 24, Y = 25, Z = 26
   D + Z = 30; W + H = 31
   P + H = 24; Z + R = 44
   O + Y = 40; X + S = 43
4. 4,613 is wrong because instead of putting 13 in the ones column, the 3 should be in the ones column and the 1 should be carried to the tens column. The correct answer is 473.
   5,107 is wrong because instead of putting 10 in the middle, the 0 should be in the tens column and the 1 should be carried to the hundreds column. The correct answer is 607.
6. Order may vary; 100, 71, 114, 82, 133, 65
8.
   165    166    167    168    169    170    171    172    173    174
 + 165  + 166  + 167  + 168  + 169  + 170  + 171  + 172  + 173  + 174
 -----  -----  -----  -----  -----  -----  -----  -----  -----  -----
   330    332    334    336    338    340    342    344    346    348
9. 48 ~~16~~ ~~32~~ 57 29 59 ~~45~~ 37
   When added to 3, the numbers in the ones place will not make a sum that needs to be regrouped.

**Page 16**

T. 418      H. 925      I. 940       O. 346
G. 877      S. 806      O. 420      E. 833
T. 701      D. 753      L. 881       H. 885
T. 653      R. 987      O. 644      E. 524

<u>TO GET TO THE OTHER SLIDE!</u>

## Page 17

2–4. Answers may vary.

1.
| 51 | 25 | 62 | 46 |
|----|----|----|----|

| 26 | 37 | 16 |
|----|----|----|

| 11 | 21 |
|----|----|

| 10 |
|----|

6.
$$\begin{array}{r} 54 \\ -29 \\ \hline 25 \end{array} \quad \begin{array}{r} 35 \\ -29 \\ \hline 6 \end{array} \quad \begin{array}{r} 62 \\ -29 \\ \hline 33 \end{array} \quad \begin{array}{r} 81 \\ -29 \\ \hline 52 \end{array}$$

7.
$$\begin{array}{r} 3\,1 \\ \cancel{4}5 \\ -18 \\ \hline 27 \end{array} \text{ or } \begin{array}{r} 3\,1 \\ \cancel{4}5 \\ -27 \\ \hline 18 \end{array} \text{ or } \begin{array}{r} 3\,1 \\ \cancel{4}5 \\ -28 \\ \hline 17 \end{array} \text{ or } \begin{array}{r} 3\,1 \\ \cancel{4}5 \\ -17 \\ \hline 28 \end{array}$$

8. $95 - 38 = 57$
9. 69, 35, 17

## Page 18

A. 37  B. 79  C. correct
D. correct  E. 18  F. correct
G. correct  H. 38  I. correct
J. correct  K. correct  L. 43

14 points

## Page 19

6–9. Answers may vary.
1. 651 won't work because the 6 in the hundreds column is larger than the 4 in the hundreds column. 203 won't work because it doesn't need regrouping. 318 doesn't work because it needs regrouping in the ones column and doesn't need regrouping in the tens or the hundreds column.

2.
$$\begin{array}{r} 841 \\ -148 \\ \hline 693 \end{array} \quad \begin{array}{r} 983 \\ -389 \\ \hline 594 \end{array} \quad \begin{array}{r} 732 \\ -237 \\ \hline 495 \end{array} \quad \begin{array}{r} 754 \\ -457 \\ \hline 297 \end{array} \quad \begin{array}{r} 652 \\ -256 \\ \hline 396 \end{array}$$

3. $627 - 253$ needs regrouping because the 5 in the tens column is larger than the 2.

4.
$$\begin{array}{r} 810 \\ -287 \\ \hline 523 \end{array} \quad \begin{array}{r} 723 \\ -287 \\ \hline 436 \end{array} \quad \begin{array}{r} 541 \\ -287 \\ \hline 254 \end{array} \quad \begin{array}{r} 302 \\ -287 \\ \hline 15 \end{array}$$

$$\begin{array}{r} 631 \\ -287 \\ \hline 344 \end{array} \quad \begin{array}{r} 456 \\ -287 \\ \hline 169 \end{array} \quad \begin{array}{r} 702 \\ -287 \\ \hline 415 \end{array} \quad \begin{array}{r} 365 \\ -287 \\ \hline 78 \end{array}$$

## Page 20

Order may vary.

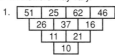
$$\begin{array}{r} 50 \\ -43 \\ \hline 7 \end{array} \quad \begin{array}{r} 50 \\ -18 \\ \hline 32 \end{array} \quad \begin{array}{r} 43 \\ -18 \\ \hline 25 \end{array}$$

$$\begin{array}{r} 72 \\ -35 \\ \hline 37 \end{array} \quad \begin{array}{r} 72 \\ -29 \\ \hline 43 \end{array} \quad \begin{array}{r} 35 \\ -29 \\ \hline 6 \end{array}$$

$$\begin{array}{r} 813 \\ -739 \\ \hline 74 \end{array} \quad \begin{array}{r} 813 \\ -464 \\ \hline 349 \end{array} \quad \begin{array}{r} 739 \\ -464 \\ \hline 275 \end{array}$$

$$\begin{array}{r} 903 \\ -651 \\ \hline 252 \end{array} \quad \begin{array}{r} 903 \\ -178 \\ \hline 725 \end{array} \quad \begin{array}{r} 651 \\ -178 \\ \hline 473 \end{array}$$

## Page 21

3, 6, 7. Answers may vary.
1. Order of addends may vary. Possible answers include $32 + 21 = 53$, $32 + 65 = 97$, $32 + 14 = 46$, $32 + 33 = 65$, $21 + 65 = 86$, $21 + 14 = 35$, $21 + 33 = 54$, $65 + 14 = 79$, $65 + 33 = 98$, $14 + 33 = 47$.
2. Order of addends may vary. Possible answers include $11 + 11 = 22$, $11 + 22 = 33$, $11 + 33 = 44$, $11 + 44 = 55$, $11 + 55 = 66$, $11 + 66 = 77$, $11 + 77 = 88$, $11 + 88 = 99$, $22 + 22 = 44$, $22 + 33 = 55$, $22 + 44 = 66$, $22 + 55 = 77$, $22 + 66 = 88$, $22 + 77 = 99$, $33 + 33 = 66$, $33 + 44 = 77$, $33 + 55 = 88$, $33 + 66 = 99$, $44 + 44 = 88$, $44 + 55 = 99$.

4.

8. $\triangle = 3$, $\heartsuit = 2$, $\maltese = 4$
9. $87 - 53 = 34$; The numbers in the tens column were subtracted incorrectly.
$38 - 15 = 23$; The numbers in the ones column were subtracted incorrectly.

## Page 22

A. 32  B. 97  C. 48
D. 12  E. 84  F. 46
G. 54  H. 61  I. 83
J. 98  K. 63  L. 99  M. 85  N. 95
O. 17  P. 20  Q. 74  R. 50  S. 49

**Peanuts**
| 9 | 8 | 4 | 8 | 3 |
| 9 | 5 | 6 | 1 | 2 |
| 2 | 0 | 9 | 7 | 4 |
| 6 | 3 | 5 | 4 | 9 |

## Page 23

1, 2, 8, 9. Answers may vary.

3.
| 24 | 53 | 32 |
|----|----|----|
| 39 | 41 | 16 |

4.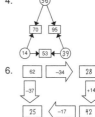

6.

7. The answer is incorrect. The correct answer is 54. Answers may vary. Possible answers include the following: solve the problem on your own, use addition, use a hundred chart, use a calculator.

## Page 24

A. 45  B. 71  C. 49  D. 25  E. 87
F. 64  G. 18  H. 91  I. 82  J. 17
K. 26  L. 30  M. 37  N. 47  O. 70

The winner is Willy.

## Page 25

1, 3, 7–9. Answers may vary.
2. 12; Answers may vary.
4.
| | Add 122. | Subtract 122. |
|-----|----------|---------------|
| 375 | 497 | 253 |
| 756 | 878 | 634 |
| 562 | 684 | 440 |
| 624 | 746 | 502 |
| 243 | 365 | 121 |

6. A. 32¢
B. 25¢
C. 24¢
D. 13¢
E. 10¢
F. 61¢

## Page 26

| 59 −43 16 | A | 197 −151 46 | E | 38 +51 89 | O |
|---|---|---|---|---|---|
| 659 −546 113 | Y | 205 +263 468 | F | 48 −20 28 | H |
| 333 −231 102 | L | 76 +22 98 | T | | |
| 65 −24 41 | V | 418 +110 528 | W | | |

THEY HAVE TWO LEFT FEET.

## Page 27

3, 4, 7, 8. Answers may vary.
1.
| | Add 126. | | Subtract 78. |
|-----|----------|-----|--------------|
| 57 | 183 | 90 | 12 |
| 84 | 210 | 165 | 87 |
| 415 | 541 | 353 | 275 |
| 780 | 906 | 502 | 424 |

2. $\$1.95 + \$1.18 = \$3.13$, $\$1.95 + \$1.27 = \$3.22$, $\$1.95 + \$1.49 = \$3.44$, $\$1.95 + \$1.66 = \$3.61$, $\$1.95 - \$1.18 = \$0.77$, $\$1.95 - \$1.27 = \$0.68$, $\$1.95 - \$1.49 = \$0.46$, $\$1.95 - \$1.66 = \$0.29$
6. 554, 819; Answers may vary.
9. 🕐 = 150. Problems will vary.

## Page 28

A.
$$\begin{array}{r} 106 \\ +57 \\ \hline 163 \end{array}$$
B.
$$\begin{array}{r} 119 \\ +57 \\ \hline 176 \end{array}$$

C.
$$\begin{array}{r} 154 \\ -148 \\ \hline 9 \end{array}$$
D.
$$\begin{array}{r} 132 \\ +119 \\ \hline 251 \end{array}$$
E.
$$\begin{array}{r} 106 \\ -57 \\ \hline 49 \end{array}$$

F.
$$\begin{array}{r} 132 \\ -106 \\ \hline 26 \end{array}$$
G.
$$\begin{array}{r} 148 \\ -119 \\ \hline 29 \end{array}$$
H.
$$\begin{array}{r} 157 \\ +148 \\ \hline 305 \end{array}$$

**Page 29**
1. Answers may vary.
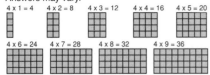
$4 \times 1 = 4$ | $4 \times 2 = 8$ | $4 \times 3 = 12$ | $4 \times 4 = 16$ | $4 \times 5 = 20$
$4 \times 6 = 24$ | $4 \times 7 = 28$ | $4 \times 8 = 32$ | $4 \times 9 = 36$

2. Answers may vary.
3. $0 \times 1 = \underline{0}$  $\underline{1} \times 1 = 1$  $2 \times \underline{1} = 2$  $\underline{3} \times 1 = 3$  $4 \times 1 = \underline{4}$  $5 \times \underline{1} = 5$
   When a number is multiplied by 1, the product is the same as the number.
4. When you multiply, look at the first factor and skip-count by that number. Look at the second factor to tell how many times to skip-count. That will give the product.
6. Any number multiplied by zero equals zero. Facts may vary.
7.

| x | 0 | 1 | 2 | 3 | 4 | 5 |
|---|---|---|---|---|---|---|
| 0 | 0 | 0 | 0 | 0 | 0 | 0 |
| 1 | 0 | 1 | 2 | 3 | 4 | 5 |
| 2 | 0 | 2 | 4 | 6 | 8 | 10 |
| 3 | 0 | 3 | 6 | 9 | 12 | 15 |
| 4 | 0 | 4 | 8 | 12 | 16 | 20 |
| 5 | 0 | 5 | 10 | 15 | 20 | 25 |

8. Answers may vary. Possible answers include skip-count by fives, multiply 6 x 5, multiply 5 x 6, and add 5 + 5 + 5 + 5 + 5 + 5.

9. 
$2 \times 6 = 12$  $2 \times 7 = 14$  $2 \times 8 = 16$  $2 \times 9 = 18$
$3 \times 6 = 18$  $3 \times 7 = 21$  $3 \times 8 = 24$  $3 \times 9 = 27$
$4 \times 6 = 24$  $4 \times 7 = 28$  $4 \times 8 = 32$  $4 \times 9 = 36$
$5 \times 6 = 30$  $5 \times 7 = 35$  $5 \times 8 = 40$  $5 \times 9 = 45$

**Page 30**
Order may vary.
A. 2 x 8, 4 x 4
B. 1 x 9, 3 x 3
C. 3 x 4, 2 x 6
D. 4 x 1, 2 x 2
E. 4 x 6, 3 x 8
F. 2 x 3, 1 x 6
G. 0 x 7, 5 x 0
H. 2 x 9, 3 x 6

**Page 31**
1, 2, 8. Answers may vary.
3. A. $3 \times 7 = 21$
   B. $2 \times 9 = 18$
   C. $5 \times 6 = 30$
   D. $3 \times 9 = 27$
   E. $4 \times 8 = 32$
   F. $4 \times 7 = 28$
4.

| x | 6 | 9 | 8 | 7 |
|---|---|---|---|---|
| 7 | 42 | 63 | 56 | 49 |
| 9 | 54 | 81 | 72 | 63 |
| 4 | 24 | 36 | 32 | 28 |
| 8 | 48 | 72 | 64 | 56 |

6. 54, 49
   56, 64
   27, 72

7. $9 \times 1 = 9$, $9 \times 2 = 18$, $9 \times 3 = 27$, $9 \times 4 = 36$, $9 \times 5 = 45$, $9 \times 6 = 54$, $9 \times 7 = 63$, $9 \times 8 = 72$, $9 \times 9 = 81$. Possible answers include the following: Each product gets larger by nine. For each product, the digit in the ones column gets smaller by one while the digit in the tens column gets larger by one. The sum of the digits in each product equals nine.

9.

| x 7 | 49 |
|---|---|
| 5 | 35 |
| 6 | 42 |
| 3 | 21 |
| 9 | 63 |

| x 9 | 54 |
|---|---|
| 3 | 27 |
| 8 | 72 |
| 4 | 36 |
| 9 | 81 |

**Page 32**
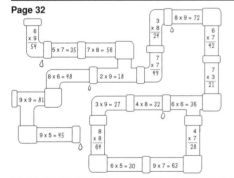
$\frac{6}{\times 9}{54}$  $8 \times 9 = 72$
$\frac{\times 8}{24}$
$\frac{7}{\times 6}{42}$
$5 \times 7 = 35$  $7 \times 8 = 56$
$\frac{7}{\times 7}{49}$
$8 \times 6 = 48$  $2 \times 9 = 18$  $\frac{7}{\times 3}{21}$
$9 \times 9 = 81$
$3 \times 9 = 27$  $4 \times 8 = 32$  $6 \times 6 = 36$
$9 \times 5 = 45$  $\frac{8}{\times 8}{64}$  $\frac{4}{\times 7}{28}$
$6 \times 5 = 30$  $9 \times 7 = 63$

**Page 33**
4, 7, 8. Answers may vary.
1. After multiplying 6 x 3, the 1 from 18 wasn't added to the product of 5 x 3.
2.  
| 14 | 21 | 44 |
|---|---|---|
| × 2 | × 3 | × 3 |
| 28 | 63 | 132 |

3.  
| 47 | 28 | 19 |
|---|---|---|
| × 2 | × 3 | × 4 |
| 94 | 84 | 76 |
| × 3 | × 3 | × 3 |
| 282 | 252 | 228 |

6. A. 68  B. 37  C. 43  D. 86
   × 3   × 5   × 8   × 4
   204   185   344   344

9. $2 \times 21 < 4 \times 11$
   $3 \times 43 > 4 \times 32$
   $3 \times 15 < 2 \times 48$

**Page 34**
A. 94
B. 304
C. 153
D. 132
E. 60
F. 408
G. 34
H. 45
I. 224
J. 108

**Page 35**
3. 8. Answers may vary.
1.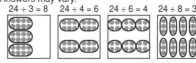
$24 \div 3 = 8$  $24 \div 4 = 6$  $24 \div 6 = 4$  $24 \div 8 = 3$

2. A number cannot be divided by 0.
4. • When a number is divided by 1, the answer will be the number.
   • When a number is divided by itself, the answer will be 1.
   Examples may vary.
6. Any number can go into the box. Zero divided by any number equals zero.
7. Students should show four of the following combinations:

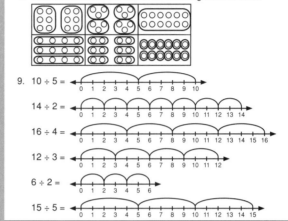

9. $10 \div 5 =$
   $14 \div 2 =$
   $16 \div 4 =$
   $12 \div 3 =$
   $6 \div 2 =$
   $15 \div 5 =$

**Page 36**
$4 \div 2 = 2$
$16 \div 4 = 4$
$5 \div 5 = 1$
$3 \div 1 = 3$
$10 \div 2 = 5$
$12 \div 4 = 3$
$25 \div 5 = 5$
$8 \div 2 = 4$
$10 \div 5 = 2$
$3 \div 3 = 1$
$4 \div 1 = 4$
$6 \div 3 = 2$
$15 \div 3 = 5$
$1 \div 1 = 1$
$9 \div 3 = 3$
$2 \div 2 = 1$
$8 \div 2 = 4$
$6 \div 2 = 3$
$20 \div 4 = 5$
$12 \div 3 = 4$

Order may vary.
1
banana
juice
wrap
cookie
2
watermelon
water
chicken
chips
3
pear
soda
bagel
cupcake
4
apple
lemonade
sandwich
doughnut
5
grapes
iced tea
salad
brownie

**Page 37**
4, 7–9. Answers may vary.
1. Answers may vary. Possible answers include the following:
   12: 12 ÷ 2 = 6, 12 ÷ 6 = 2, 12 ÷ 3 = 4, 12 ÷ 4 = 3, 12 ÷ 1 = 12
   16: 16 ÷ 2 = 8, 16 ÷ 8 = 2, 16 ÷ 4 = 4
   18: 18 ÷ 2 = 9, 18 ÷ 9 = 2, 18 ÷ 6 = 3, 18 ÷ 3 = 6
   24: 24 ÷ 3 = 8, 24 ÷ 8 = 3, 24 ÷ 6 = 4, 24 ÷ 4 = 6
   36: 36 ÷ 4 = 9, 36 ÷ 9 = 4, 36 ÷ 6 = 6
2. 21 ÷ 7 = 3, 49 ÷ 7 = 7, 42 ÷ 7 = 6, 63 ÷ 7 = 9, 56 ÷ 7 = 8, 14 ÷ 7 = 2, 7 ÷ 7 = 1, 35 ÷ 7 = 5, 28 ÷ 7 = 4
3. 

| Evenly Divisible by 4 | Both | Evenly Divisible by 6 |
|---|---|---|
| 16 | 12 | 6 |
| 20 | 24 | 18 |
| 28 | 36 | 30 |
| 32 | | 42 |

6. 7, 6, 42: 42 ÷ 6 = 7 or 42 ÷ 7 = 6
   36, 9, 4, 36 ÷ 9 = 4 or 36 ÷ 4 = 9
   4, 32, 8: 32 ÷ 8 = 4 or 32 ÷ 4 = 8
   54, 9, 6: 54 ÷ 9 = 6 or 54 ÷ 6 = 9

**Page 38**

| | |
|---|---|
| 30 ÷ 6 = 5 | 5 T |
| 49 ÷ 7 = 7 | 7 H |
| 27 ÷ 9 = 3 | 3 E |
| 72 ÷ 9 = 8 | 8 Y |
| 54 ÷ 6 = 9 | 9 A |
| 42 ÷ 7 = 6 | 6 R |
| 35 ÷ 5 = 7 | 7 E |
| 64 ÷ 8 = 8 | 8 S |
| 36 ÷ 6 = 6 | 6 M |
| 45 ÷ 9 = 5 | 9 A |
| 48 ÷ 8 = 6 | 6 R |
| 18 ÷ 9 = 2 | 2 T |
| 28 ÷ 7 = 4 | 4 K |
| 24 ÷ 6 = 4 | 6 I |
| 56 ÷ 8 = 7 | 7 D |
| 16 ÷ 4 = 4 | 4 S |

THEY ARE SMART KIDS!

**Page 39**
2–4, 9. Answers may vary.
1. A. 63 ÷ 7 = 9; 7 x 9 = 63   B. 56 ÷ 8 = 7; 8 x 7 = 56
   C. 42 ÷ 6 = 7; 6 x 7 = 42   D. 27 ÷ 3 = 9; 3 x 9 = 27
   E. 32 ÷ 4 = 8; 4 x 8 = 32   F. 45 ÷ 5 = 9; 5 x 9 = 45
6. 2, 9, 18: 2 x 9 = 18; 9 x 2 = 18; 18 ÷ 2 = 9; 18 ÷ 9 = 2
   3, 8, 24: 3 x 8 = 24; 8 x 3 = 24; 24 ÷ 3 = 8; 24 ÷ 8 = 3
   4, 5, 20: 4 x 5 = 20; 5 x 4 = 20; 20 ÷ 4 = 5; 20 ÷ 5 = 4
   5, 7, 35: 5 x 7 = 35; 7 x 5 = 35; 35 ÷ 5 = 7; 35 ÷ 7 = 5
7. Answers may vary but should include that products and quotients are answers to math problems, but that products are answers to multiplication problems and quotients are answers to division problems.
8. 4 x 7 = 28   36 ÷ 6 = 6   8 x 8 = 64
   72 ÷ 9 = 8   5 x 6 = 30   9 x 4 = 36
   9 x 9 = 81   25 ÷ 5 = 5   3 x 4 = 12
   14 ÷ 2 = 7   3 x 8 = 24   6 ÷ 6 = 1

**Page 40**
Across
A. 12
C. 40
E. 36
G. 45
I. 48
K. 16
M. 30
O. 72
Q. 2
S. 42
Down
B. 24
D. 3
F. 64
H. 54
J. 81
L. 63
N. 7
P. 20
R. 24
T. 27

## Page 41

1, 6, 9. Answers may vary.
2. 168, 248, 328, 408, 488, 568. Each problem has 1 and 8 in the ones column, so each answer has 8 in the ones column. Each problem has one more ten than the problem before it, so each answer is 80 more than the one before it.
3. A remainder is the amount left over when a number cannot be divided equally. 2)87 will have a remainder because 7 cannot be divided into two equal groups.
4. 15 x 5 = 75, the numbers in the ones column were added, not multiplied; 144 ÷ 3 = 48, 3 goes into 24 eight times; 26 x 4 = 104, the child multiplied 2 x 4, and then multiplied that product by 2 instead of adding; 120 ÷ 5 = 24, the child did not bring down the zero before dividing again.
7. 42 x 4 = 168, 168 ÷ 4 = 42. Answers on the T chart will vary. Possible answers include the following: Alike—use the same numbers; all numbers are even. Different—one problem is multiplication and the other is division; the multiplication problem has a much larger answer.
8. 165 ÷ 5 = 33, 237 ÷ 3 = 79, 248 ÷ 4 = 62, 192 ÷ 6 = 32

## Page 42

A. 57    B. 155    C. 64
D. 104   E. 40     F. 35
G. 76    H. 78
I. 92    J. 159
K. 205   L. 81

## Page 43

7, 9. Answers may vary.
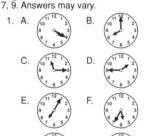
2. A. 3:30
   B. 9:00
   C. 5:15
   D. 6:45
   E. 12:00
3. A. 1:50      B. 10:45
   C. 5:10      D. 6:30
   E. 8:55      F. 9:20
   G. 2:25      H. 12:05
   I. 3:35      J. 6:00
4. Drawings will vary.
   A. 7:00 AM    B. 3:00 PM
   C. 7:00 PM    D. 3:00 AM
6.  1:45, 2:00, 2:15, 2:30, 2:45,
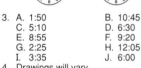 3:00, 3:15, 3:30
8. Answers may vary but should reflect that clocks do not show 60 minutes, even though there are 60 minutes in an hour. The clock should show 4:00.

## Page 44

A. 2:20   B. 2:30   C. 2:40   D. 2:50   E. 3:00

F. 7:15   G. 7:45   H. 8:15   I. 8:45   J. 9:15

K. 10:00  L. 10:20  M. 10:40  N. 11:00  O. 11:20

## Page 45

2, 3, 8. Answers may vary.
1. It is about 12:45. The hour hand is closer to the 1 than to the 12.

4. 1:23   2:34   3:45   4:56

6. 1:59   3:11

7. A. 3:02      E. 11:33
   B. 5:46      F. 9:21
   C. 8:29      G. 12:17
   D. 7:06      H. 2:34

9.  1:11   2:22   3:33   4:44   5:55

## Page 46

| 9:11 | 6:43 | 1:26 | 10:32 | 4:57 |

| 2:38 | 7:51 | 12:14 | 3:49 | 8:24 |

## Page 47

1. A. one quarter, one dime, one nickel, three pennies
   B. one half-dollar, one quarter, three pennies
   C. one half-dollar, one quarter, one dime, one nickel
   D. two dimes, two pennies
   E. one quarter, one penny
   F. one half-dollar, one nickel, one penny
   G. one dime, four pennies
   H. one half-dollar, one dime, one nickel
2. A. nickel = 20 nickels
   B. quarter = 4 quarters
   C. penny = 100 pennies
   D. dime = 10 dimes
3. Answers may vary. Possible answers include the following: five dimes, one nickel; eleven nickels; two quarters, one nickel; one quarter, six nickels; and one quarter, three dimes.
4.
| Price | Paid | Change |
|-------|------|--------|
| 29¢ | 50¢ | 21¢ |
| 77¢ | $1.00 | 23¢ |
| 56¢ | 75¢ | 19¢ |
| 18¢ | 50¢ | 32¢ |
| 35¢ | $1.00 | 65¢ |

6. 6 nickels = 3 dimes
   2 quarters = 50 pennies
   6 dimes = 12 nickels
   15 nickels = 3 quarters
   16 nickels = 8 dimes
   75 pennies = 15 nickels

7. one quarter, four dimes, one nickel, two pennies
8. A. 60¢   B. 70¢   C. 59¢   D. 80¢   E. 45¢
9. One quarter, two dimes; one quarter, one dime, two nickels; one quarter, four nickels; four dimes, one nickel; three dimes, three nickels; two dimes, five nickels; one dime, seven nickels; nine nickels

## Page 48

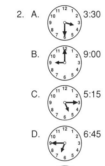

## Page 49

4, 6, 7, 9. Answers may vary.
1.
|  | 2 | 3 | 5 | 6 |
|--|---|---|---|---|
| penny | 2¢ | 3¢ | 5¢ | 6¢ |
| nickel | 10¢ | 15¢ | 25¢ | 30¢ |
| dime | 20¢ | 30¢ | 50¢ | 60¢ |
| quarter | 50¢ | 75¢ | $1.25 | $1.50 |

2. four dollar bills, two quarters; three dollar bills, six quarters; two dollar bills, ten quarters; one dollar bill, fourteen quarters; eighteen quarters
3. the ball ($1.37), the bear ($1.92), and the crayons ($1.71)

8. A. $3.25   B. $2.70   C. $1.02   D. 76¢   E. $4.14

## Page 50

A. $4.17, hot dog        B. $3.06, cotton candy
C. $2.80, pretzel        D. $2.37, popcorn
E. $4.27, cheeseburger   F. $3.63, nachos

## Page 52

A. 5 in.; 13 cm   D. 4 in.; 9 cm    G. 0 in.; 1 cm    J. 1 in.; 3 cm
B. 1 in.; 3 cm    E. 6 in.; 14 cm   H. 4 in.; 11 cm   K. 2 in.; 6 cm
C. 0 in.; 1 cm    F. 2 in.; 4 cm    I. 1 in.; 4 cm    L. 2 in.; 5 cm

## Page 53

1, 2, 4, 6–9. Answers may vary.
3. A. 24 cm; 8 in.   B. 72 cm; 28 in.   C. 100 cm; 40 in.

## Page 54

A. 4½ in.; 11½ cm   C. 4½ in.; 11 cm   E. 5 in.; 12½ cm   G. 3 in.; 8 cm
B. 7 in.; 17½ cm   D. 5½ in.; 14 cm   F. 8 in.; 20 cm   H. 6 in.; 15 cm

## Page 55

3, 4, 6–8. Answers may vary.
1. pool—gallons
   sink—quarts, gallons
   fishbowl—pints, quarts
   bathtub—gallons
   teacup—cups
   bucket—pints, quarts
   pitcher—pints, quarts
   vase—cups, quarts

2. 2 quarts = <u>8</u> cups
   3 pints = <u>6</u> cups
   8 quarts = <u>2</u> gallons
   8 pints = <u>4</u> quarts
   1 gallon = <u>16</u> pints
   4 cups = <u>1</u> quart

9. A. one quart
   B. one pint
   C. one quart
   D. one cup
   E. one pint

## Page 56

A.
| pints | 1 | 2 | 3 | 4 | 5 | 6 |
|---|---|---|---|---|---|---|
| cups | 2 | 4 | 6 | 8 | 10 | 12 |

B.
| gallons | 1 | 2 | 3 | 4 | 5 | 6 |
|---|---|---|---|---|---|---|
| quarts | 4 | 8 | 12 | 16 | 20 | 24 |

C.
| quarts | 1 | 2 | 3 | 4 | 5 | 6 |
|---|---|---|---|---|---|---|
| pints | 2 | 4 | 6 | 8 | 10 | 12 |

D.
| gallons | 1 | 2 | 3 | 4 | 5 | 6 |
|---|---|---|---|---|---|---|
| pints | 8 | 16 | 24 | 32 | 40 | 48 |

E.
| quarts | 1 | 2 | 3 | 4 | 5 | 6 |
|---|---|---|---|---|---|---|
| cups | 4 | 8 | 12 | 16 | 20 | 24 |

F.
| gallons | 1 | 2 | 3 | 4 | 5 | 6 |
|---|---|---|---|---|---|---|
| cups | 16 | 32 | 48 | 64 | 80 | 96 |

## Page 57

1–4, 8, 9. Answers may vary.
6.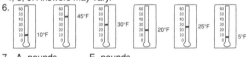
   45°F   30°F   20°F   25°F
   10°F   5°F

7. A. pounds   E. pounds
   B. ounces   F. pounds
   C. pounds   G. ounces
   D. ounces   H. ounces

## Page 58

A. 60°, Thurs.   C. 55°, Tues.   E. 40°, Sun.   G. 75°, Sat.
B. 65°, Fri.   D. 50°, Mon.   F. 45°, Wed.

## Page 59

4, 9. Answers may vary.
1. A. 3, 6, 9, 12, 15, 18, 21, 24, 27
   B. 20, 25, 30, 35, 40, 45, 50, 55, 60
   C. 90, 80, 70, 60, 50, 40, 30, 20, 10
   D. 1, 4, 9, 16, 25, 36, 49, 64, 81
   E. 31, 29, 27, 25, 23, 21, 19, 17, 15
2. It will be sunny. The odd days are sunny and the even days are rainy.
3. A, B, C, and E should be circled.
6. A. + 2   B. − 3   C. + 10   D. + 50, + 500, + 5,000, etc.   E. − 10
7.
| Cars | 1 | 2 | 3 | 4 | 5 | 6 |
|---|---|---|---|---|---|---|
| Wheels | 4 | 8 | 12 | 16 | 20 | 24 |

8. Answers may vary. Possible answers include when multiplying, when adding, when playing games, when measuring, when building with blocks, and when writing poetry.

## Page 60

A. 14, 17, <u>20</u>, <u>23</u>, 26, 29, <u>32</u>, 35, 38
   Rule: add 3
B. <u>16</u>, 14, 12, 10, <u>8</u>, <u>6</u>, <u>4</u>, 2, 0
   Rule: subtract 2 or count back by 2
C. 3, 5, 8, 3, 5, 8, <u>3</u>, <u>5</u>, <u>8</u>
   Rule: repeat 3, 5, 8

D. 45, <u>50</u>, 55, 60, 65, <u>70</u>, <u>75</u>, 80, 85
   Rule: count by 5s
E. 1, 2, 4, 8, 16, <u>32</u>, <u>64</u>, <u>128</u>, 256
   Rule: double the number or multiply by 2
F. 51, <u>47</u>, <u>43</u>, 39, 35, 31, 27, <u>23</u>, 19
   Rule: subtract 4

## Page 61

3, 4, 7, 9. Answers will vary.
1.
| Figure | Number of Triangles | Number of Lines (\\) |
|---|---|---|
| | 1 | 3 |
| | 2 | 5 |
| | 3 | 7 |
| | 4 | 9 |
| | 5 | 11 |
| | 6 | 13 |
| | 7 | 15 |

2. Each square in the pattern is shown four times.

6.

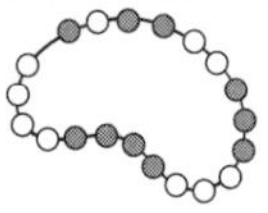

8. A. ▲ ● ● ▲ ☒ ● ▲ ● or ▲ ☒ ● ▲ ■ ● ▲
   B. ■ ▲ ● ■ ▲ ● ☒
   C. ☒ ■ ● ■ ■ ● ■ ■

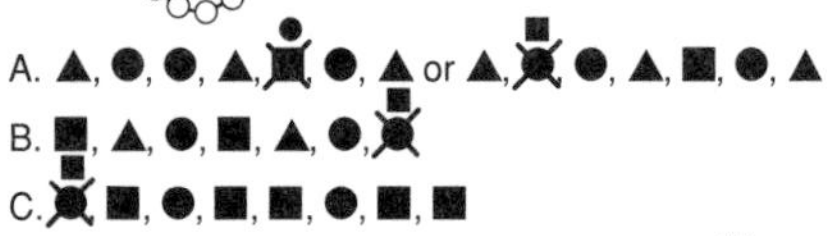

## Page 62

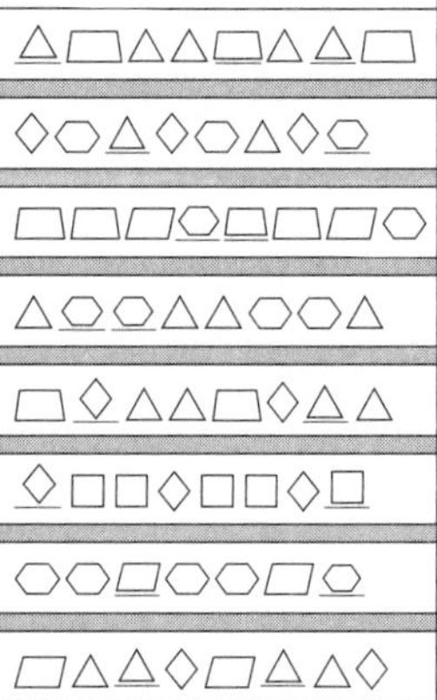

| | Pattern | Rule Number |
|---|---|---|
| A. | △ ▱ △ ▱ △ ▱ | 2 |
| B. | ◇ ▱ △ ◇ ▱ ⬡ | 4 |
| C. | ▭ ▱ ▱ ◯ ▭ ▱ | 5 |
| D. | △ ◯ ⬡ △ ◯ △ | 8 |
| E. | ▭ ◇ △ △ ◇ △ △ | 7 |
| F. | ◇ ▭ ▱ ◇ ▭ ▱ ◇ ▭ | 3 |
| G. | ⬡ ◇ ▱ ⬡ ◇ ▱ ◯ | 1 |
| H. | ▱ △ ◇ ▱ ▱ △ ◇ | 6 |

## Page 63

1. It shows that the sum is the same even when the order of the addends changes.
2. You can use the commutative property. Then you'll know that when the order of the addends is switched, the sum is the same.
3. (7 + 3) + 4 = 14, 7 + (3 + 4) = 14; The problems show that, no matter how you group the addends, the sum is the same.
4. The associative property deals with grouping addends, so *grouping property* is another good name for it.
6. When you add 0, the answer is always the other addend.
7. A number line shows that, no matter which way you group the factors when you multiply, the product is the same.
8. The arrays show that, no matter which way the factors are grouped, the product is the same.
9. 8 x 1 = 8        1 x 7 = 7
   5 x 1 = 5        4 x 1 = 4
   1 x 9 = 9        1 x 2 = 2
   When you multiply by 1, the answer is always the other factor.

## Page 64

A. 3 x 7 = 21   B. 8 x 6 = 48   C. 5 x 2 = 10
   7 x 3 = 21      6 x 8 = 48      2 x 5 = 10
D. 9 x 7 = 63   E. 3 x 4 = 12   F. 6 x 7 = 42
   7 x 9 = 63      4 x 3 = 12      7 x 6 = 42
G. 6 x 3 = 18   H. 9 x 5 = 45   I. 4 x 7 = 28
   3 x 6 = 18      5 x 9 = 45      7 x 4 = 28
J. 2 x 8 = 16   K. 1 x 9 = 9    L. 5 x 3 = 15
   8 x 2 = 16      9 x 1 = 9       3 x 5 = 15

## Page 65

4, 7, 8. Answers may vary.
1. 22; Number riddles may vary.
2. 7 + <u>3</u> = 6 + 4
   8 + 3 = <u>5</u> + 6
   5 + 5 = 2 + <u>8</u>
   9 + <u>5</u> = 6 + 8
   <u>4</u> + 8 = 7 + 5
3. 3 + 3 + 4 + 4 − 5 − 5 = 4

6. Answers may vary. Possible solutions include the following:

| 6 | 1 | 8 | | 6 | 7 | 2 |
|---|---|---|---|---|---|---|
| 7 | 5 | 3 | | 1 | 5 | 9 |
| 2 | 9 | 4 | | 8 | 3 | 4 |

9.

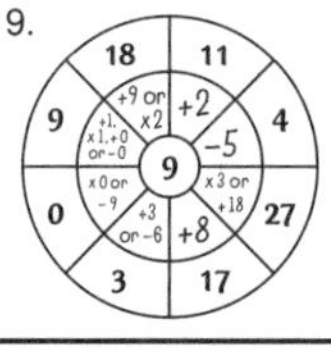

## Page 66

A. 12 − <u>7</u> = 5   F. 16 − 8 = <u>8</u>   K. <u>8</u> + 6 = 14   P. 6 + 4 = 10
B. 5 + <u>9</u> = 14   G. 5 + <u>6</u> = 11   L. <u>10</u> − 6 = 4      10 = 4 + 6 or 10 − 4 = 6
C. 15 − <u>9</u> = 6   H. 7 + <u>4</u> = 11   M. 12 − 4 = <u>8</u>   Q. 15 = 7 + 8 or 15 − 7 = 8
D. 8 + <u>7</u> = 15   I. <u>16</u> − 6 = 10   N. 7 + <u>7</u> = 14      8 + 7 = 15
E. 5 − <u>5</u> = 0    J. 12 − <u>4</u> = 8   O. <u>9</u> + 6 = 15   R. 13 = 5 + 8 or 13 − 5 = 8
                                                                         13 = 8 + 5 or 13 − 8 = 5
                                                                      S. 12 = 8 + 4 or 12 − 8 = 4
                                                                         8 + 4 = 12
                                                                      T. 5 + 6 = 11
                                                                         11 = 6 + 5 or 11 − 6 = 5

## Page 67

1–4, 6, 7. Answers may vary.
8.

In the second figure, the sections are not the same size.

9.
| Folds | Sections | Number Sentence |
|---|---|---|
| 1 | 2 | ½ + ½ = 1 |
| 2 | 4 | ¼ + ¼ + ¼ + ¼ = 1 |
| 3 | 8 | ⅛ + ⅛ + ⅛ + ⅛ + ⅛ + ⅛ + ⅛ + ⅛ = 1 |
| 4 | 16 | 1/16 + 1/16 + 1/16 + 1/16 + 1/16 + 1/16 + 1/16 + 1/16 + 1/16 + 1/16 + 1/16 + 1/16 + 1/16 + 1/16 + 1/16 + 1/16 = 1 |

**Page 68**
Order of colors may vary. The following colored sections should be shown:
A. one blue, two yellow
B. one blue, one yellow, two red
C. three blue, one yellow, two red
D. four blue, five yellow, three red
E. five yellow, five red
F. two blue, four yellow, three red
G. six blue, two red
H. two blue, two yellow, one red
I. three blue, two yellow, two red

**Page 69**
4, 9. Answers may vary.
1. A. ½ B. 2/4 or ½ C. 3/6 or ½
2. One-half should be crossed out. It is the only fraction that does not have the same denominator as another fraction. Also, each of the fractions with the same denominator can be paired to equal one whole.
3. ½, 2/4; 2/8, 1/4; 2/6, 1/3; 1/5, 2/10; 1/6, 2/12
6. 4/8; Fractions may vary.
7. A. shaded = 0.3, unshaded = 0.7
   B. shaded = 0.6, unshaded = 0.4
   C. shaded = 0.1, unshaded = 0.9
   D. shaded = 0.8, unshaded = 0.2
8.

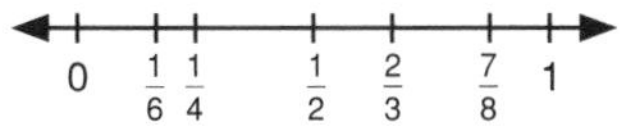
0
1/6
1/4
1/2
2/3
7/8
1

**Page 70**
2/6 1/2 2/4 7/8 2/3 3/4 1/3

| | | | |
|---|---|---|---|
| A. > | B. > | C. < | D. < |
| E. > | F. < | G. = | H. > |
| I. = | J. < | K. > | L. > |
| M. < | N. < | O. > | P. > |

**Page 71**
2, 4, 6, 7. Answers may vary.
1. Snow Cones Sold on Friday

| | |
|---|---|
| After Lunch | 卌 卌 II |
| After Dinner | 卌 卌 卌 卌 IIII |

3. A title is missing. It is needed so the reader knows what the data is showing.
8. Winnie made more snow cones. When the tallies are added, Winnie made 24 snow cones and Will made 23.
9. data: information collected
   graph: a diagram to show data
   survey: a method of gathering information
   tally: a mark used to record data on a tally chart

**Page 72**
Saturday Snow Cone Sales

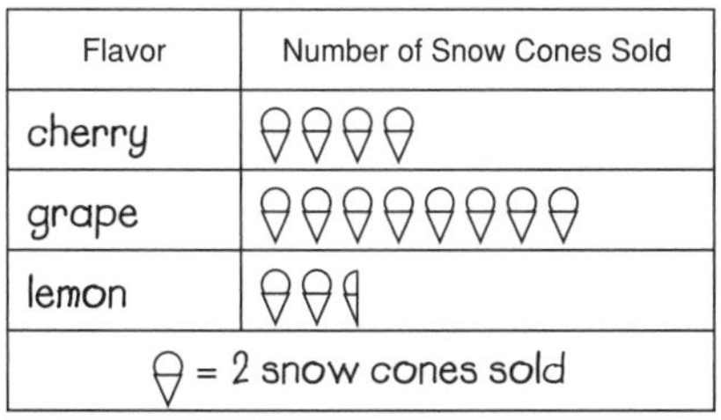
Flavor
Number of Snow Cones Sold
cherry
grape
lemon
= 2 snow cones sold

Sentences will vary.

**Page 73**
1, 2, 4, 7. Answers may vary.
3. Answers may vary. The labels on the side and bottom would be switched. The data and title would be the same.
6. Favorite Food Flavors

| | |
|---|---|
| beef | 卌 卌 卌 卌 IIII |
| tuna | 卌 卌 卌 卌 卌 卌 卌 |
| chicken | 卌 卌 卌 I |
| salmon | 卌 卌 卌 卌 卌 卌 III |

8.

| Pictographs | Both | Bar Graphs |
|---|---|---|
| show pictures | show data | show bars |
| have a key | have titles | have numbered scales |
| | can be organized in rows or columns | |

9. Answers may vary. Items on list may include the following: title, tells what the graph is about; labels, tell what kind of data is shown; scale, units used; bars or lines and points or pictures, show the data; key, tells how many each picture represents.

**Page 74**

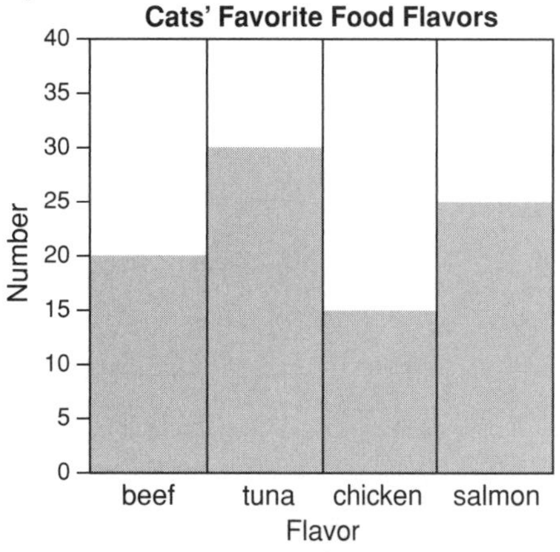
Cats' Favorite Food Flavors
Number
0
5
10
15
20
25
30
35
40
beef
tuna
chicken
salmon
Flavor

A. 30
B. 15
C. salmon
D. 15
E. 10
F. 90

**Page 75**
1, 2, 6, 7. Answers may vary.

3. I would most likely pick a polka-dotted hat because there are four of them and only one plaid and one striped hat.
4. It is most likely I will pick 8. It is least likely I will pick 6. It is certain I will pick an even number.
8. It is possible to eat a pizza. *true*
   It is possible to hear a pizza. *false*
   It is impossible to see a mouse. *false*
   It is impossible to see a mouse fly. *true*
9. All three cubes should be blue in the first bag. Three of the four cubes should be red in the second bag. None of the cubes in the third bag should be green.

**Page 76**
1. No; to be a fair spinner, this spinner should have equal sections.
2. pepperoni
3. sausage
4. certain
5. impossible

Spins will vary.

6. Answers may vary.

**Page 77**
1, 4, 6, 8, 9. Answers may vary.
2. 14 squares, 22 rectangles
3. six triangles =

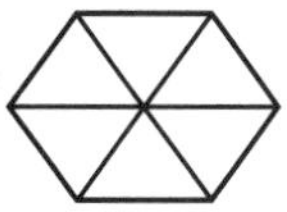

two trapezoids =

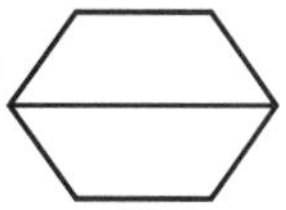

two rhombuses and two triangles =

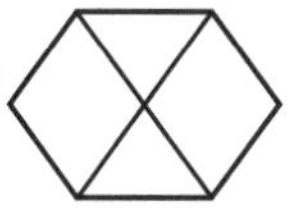

7. No Lines of Symmetry: F, G, J, L, N, P, Q, R, S, Z
   One Line of Symmetry: A, B, C, D, E, K, M, T, U, V, W, Y
   Two or More Lines of Symmetry: H, I, O, X

**Page 78**
Shapes A and D are congruent shapes. This means they are the same size and shape. Shapes B and C are also congruent. If you move shapes B and C together to make one shape, that new shape would be congruent to shape E. You could also put shapes B and C together in a different way to make them congruent to shape G.
Shapes A, B, C, D, and F each have one line of symmetry. If you take a look at shape G, you will see that it has two lines of symmetry. Shape E does not have any lines of symmetry.

**Page 79**
1–4, 6, 8. Answers may vary.
7. A cube has 6 faces, 8 vertices, and 12 edges. Two cubes put together would make a rectangular prism, which also has 6 faces, 8 vertices, and 12 edges.
9. Right angles traced may vary.

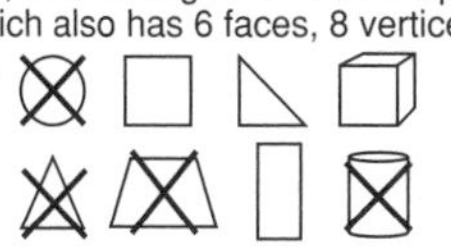

**Page 80**

| Plane Shape Face | Solid Figure | Solid Figure Description |
|---|---|---|
| 1. circle | cone | 1 face<br>1 vertex<br>1 edge |
| 2. square | cube | 6 faces<br>8 vertices<br>12 edges |
| 3. triangle | triangular pyramid | 4 faces<br>4 vertices<br>6 edges |
| 4. rectangle | rectangular prism | 6 faces<br>8 vertices<br>12 edges |
| 5. oval | cylinder | 2 faces<br>0 vertices<br>2 edges |

**Page 81**
1. 75 stones
2. two female crows: 10
   four female crows: 20
   eight female crows: 40
3. Jim, Hal, Cal, Pat, Ty
4. Answers may vary.
6. Answers may vary. The number of nuts Crow ate first is missing. Without that number, the total cannot be found.
7. 70 minutes; Explanations will vary but may include the following: skip-count by ten seven times; add 10 + 10 + 10 + 10 + 10 + 10 + 10; use a hundred chart, start at 10, and count down seven rows to 70.
8. six pairs of birds: crow, jay; crow, finch; crow, robin; jay, finch; jay, robin; finch, robin
9. Answers may vary but should include the following: Start at 44 and move up one row to 34 to subtract ten. Move left across the row three spaces. Then go up to the right side of the row above. Count back three more spaces. The answer is 27 twigs.

**Page 82**
A.
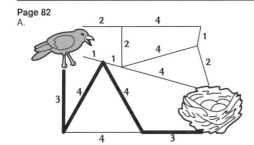
B.

| Day | Mon. | Tues. | Wed. | Thurs. | Fri. |
|---|---|---|---|---|---|
| Miles | 4 | 7 | 10 | 13 | 16 |

C. 54 stones, 11:30
D. 6 more nuts
E. 80 friends; The answer would be the same because the problem uses the same tens-place digits, just in a different order.

**Page 83**
1.

| 50 | **34** | 16 |
|---|---|---|
| **30** | 42 | 28 |
| 20 | 24 | **56** |

2. 18, 36, 54, 72, 90
3. He will learn 39 tricks on Thursday and 47 tricks on Friday.
4.
6. Answers may vary.
7. He can make 9 piles of 100. He will need 28 more bones to make another pile of 100 bones. Explanations may vary.
8. It will be Saturday, April 23. Explanations may vary.
9. Drawings will vary. Each dog will have 4 toys.

**Page 84**
A. 70
B. 61
C. 822
D. 534
E. 52

**Page 85**
1. Percy, May 6; Porky, May 14; Penny, May 19; Prissy, June 2.
2. It could be a square pyramid or a cube. It could not be a cylinder, rectangular prism, or sphere.
3. perimeter = 42 feet, area = 104 square feet
4. There are nine cookies in each group with two left.
6. three yards, 108 inches
7. Order of pairs may vary. Porky and Prissy, Porky and Penny, Porky and Percy, Prissy and Penny, Prissy and Percy, Penny and Percy
8. Percy has four feet. On each foot, he has four toes. Percy also has a tail. How many toes does Percy have in all? He has 16 toes.
9. Penny watches 6/12, or 1/2; Porky watches 2/12, or 1/6; and Prissy watches 4/12, or 1/3.

**Page 86**
A. 424
B. 263
C. 567
D. 20
E. 97
F. 46
G. 50
H. 1,254

**Page 87**
1.
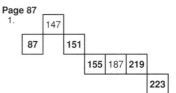
2. Orientations may vary.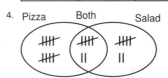
3. ten ways

| Quarters | Dimes | Nickels |
|---|---|---|
| 2 | 0 | 0 |
| 1 | 1 | 3 |
| 1 | 2 | 1 |
| 0 | 1 | 8 |
| 0 | 2 | 6 |
| 0 | 3 | 4 |
| 0 | 4 | 2 |
| 0 | 5 | 0 |
| 1 | 0 | 5 |
| 0 | 0 | 10 |

4. Pizza   Both   Salad
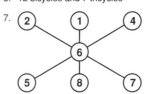
6. 12 bicycles and 7 tricycles
7.
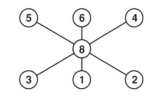
8. five vans; Explanations may vary.
9. two dimes, two quarters, and two nickels.

**Page 88**
A. 22 years
B. eight outfits
C. six days
D. $283.83
E. 228 beach visitors
F. Dan
G. six kayaks, yes
H. nine pairs